Dear Wife,

The Civil War Letters of a Private Soldier

Edited by
Jack C. Davis

THE SULGRAVE PRESS
Louisville, KY

Copyright © by Jack C. Davis

All rights reserved. No part of this book may be reproduced or transmitted in any form or by any means without written permission from the publisher, except for brief quotations in critical reviews or articles.

LIBRARY OF CONGRESS
CATALOGING-IN-PUBLICATION DATA
Davis, Jack C.
Dear Wife
Title No. 91-067904

cover design; bill swearingen
typeset design; sue dawson

THE SULGRAVE PRESS
2005 Longest Avenue
Louisville, KY 40204

ISBN 0-9624086-4-6

DEDICATION

This book is dedicated to the memory of Eva Howard Farrington, who carried the spirit of Delaware County with her throughout her long life.

Acknowledgments

This book could not have been completed without the hard work of my aunt, Doris Farrington Roberts. Her enthusiastic interest and continued support for this project, backed-up by the long hours she spent transcribing letters and researching family documents, are truly appreciated.

I owe a debt of gratitude to Herb Crumb of Norwich, New York who lent a valuable and rare book to someone he did not know and had never met.

Tom Flannery, Town of Colchester Historian, and Marion Peterson, Town of Hamden Historian, Delaware County, New York, deserve my thanks for doing some tedious research through dusty files.

And, to Jennifer Ambrose of the Delaware County Historical Association and Linda Ogborn of the County Clerk's Office, my appreciation for guiding me through their records.

Photo Credits

Many of the photographs were provided by Michael Taylor, Director of the Museum of Hilton Head Island. Mike's enthusiasm and broad-based intellectual curiosity will make the museum there a truly informative place to visit.

Tom Flannery, Town of Colchester Historian, provided the photograph of the Downsville veterans.

The Filson Club of Louisville, Kentucky provided the map for the back cover.

Jack C Davis

Contents

Page

Introduction ix

Editor's Note xvi

Chapters

Dear Friend 1

I Am A Soldier Now 16

It Is A Cold Winter In South Carolina 56

Merry Christmas 110

The Deserters 147

Surrender And Home 214

INTRODUCTION

This is not a book just about the Civil War. It is a book about one man, Daniel B. White, and about his experiences, observations, thoughts, and feelings during the eleven months in 1864 and 1865 when he served in the 144th New York State Volunteer Infantry. Through letters to his wife, Daniel tells us today what his life was like for that one year almost 130 years ago.

Through his eyes we can not only see the day-to-day life of an infantry private soldier with all the tedium and sacrifice that service required, but we also gain some appreciation for the life he led before and after the war and how that now nearly vanished way of life was woven into the fabric of Northern society.

Daniel's war was not an exciting war or even a particularly dangerous one. He served at Hilton Head, South Carolina, building fortifications, guarding Confederate prisoners, and standing sentry duty. We have no reason to believe he was ever under fire, or ever fired his weapon in anger. The war seemed to swirl around Daniel. Friends were sent on dangerous duty, skirmishes and battles were fought nearby, but he was not asked to participate. Instead, he did the humble duty that was required of him, and he wrote letters.

DEAR WIFE

He wrote about his daily life, the food he ate, the hours he worked, the way he lived, and he wrote incessantly about his health and the health of his friends and acquaintances. It was a rare letter, whether written by Daniel or any other person of the period, that didn't mention the health of the writer and offer wishes of good health to the recipient and his or her family. And little wonder, during nearly three years of service the 144th lost 178 officers and men to disease while losing 39 to wounds received in battle, a ratio of better than four to one. Some other regiments had similar records, but sources indicate that for the total Union army the ratio of "Dead from Disease" to "Killed in Action" was somewhere between two and three to one.

His emotions bubble near the surface of his writing, sometimes breaking through to express his longing for his wife, Amanda, and his home, sometimes to express fear. Although he was not called on to go into battle, he never knew when it might happen. Other companies of the 144th were sent off to the battle of Honey Hill and engagements at Deveaux Neck and Tullifinney River, while Daniel and the rest of Company K stayed at Hilton Head to maintain order and guard prisoners. The question of whether he would be sent to join them was never far from his mind or his writing.

Daniel's humor often comes through. There is a touchingly told, self deprecating story of Amanda's prowess at selling sheep, and another rather coarse story about his encounter with two young women who visited the camp. Mainly, however, his humor asserts itself through sly comments, some with a bit of an edge, that, when read within the body of his collected letters, tell us something of his personality.

Daniel saw some of the ugliness of war at first hand. His descriptions of the conditions under which Confederate prisoners were kept can be chilling to us today, but Daniel rarely shows any feeling on the subject. In fact, though he mentions the "Rebs" frequently, he never uses the name of one of the Confederate prisoners he encountered. We don't know whether he did not know the names or did not care to tell them.

Hilton Head, South Carolina during 1864 and 1865 was just about the best duty a Union soldier could draw. The Port Royal area, of which Hilton Head was a part, had been captured by Union forces in late 1861 in a well planned and rather elegant maneuver. Commodore Samuel F. duPont, in charge of the operation, sailed his 17 warships in a circular pattern, firing continuous broadsides into Fort Walker on the Hilton Head side of the harbor and Fort Beauregard on the other. This constant bombardment severely overmatched the Confederate garrisons in both forts, and enabled the 12,000 Union soldiers under the command of Brigadier General Thomas W. Sherman to go ashore and secure the forts and much of the perimeter of the harbor.

Port Royal Sound was the best natural harbor on the southeastern coast with the exception of Charleston, and its capture gave the Union a stronghold from which to enforce the blockade on Confederate ports. Hilton Head became a major repair and refitting area for the ships maintaining the blockade and a center for the distribution of supplies and men to the Union forces operating in the south. Later, it also served as a collection point for Confederate prisoners.

On the eastern point of Hilton Head Island near Fort Walker (renamed Fort Welles for the Union Secretary of the Navy) there grew a small, well-outfitted community and shops along "Robber's Row", where just about anything a soldier desired could be bought, if he had the money. The prices for most items were exorbitant. Daniel tells us a little of his experiences there.

While many soldiers of both armies were on the move during much of the year, marching from one battle or skirmish to the next and foraging for adequate food, dealing with badly abused feet, carrying only what they absolutely needed, Daniel lived in relative comfort at Hilton Head. In the first few months of his stay there, he shared a tent with a few of his friends. Later on he occupied larger quarters with a stove for warmth. While others had, in many cases, inadequate clothing, Daniel stated in a letter to his brother-in-law that he had "more clothes and better than I ever had at one time in my life before."

Like all soldiers throughout history, Daniel complained about the food, the doctors, his living conditions, the delays in receiving mail and pay, and his officers. But, at some point in the winter of 1864, he began to recognize his lot was far better than that drawn by most soldiers of this period. After the battle of Honey Hill, in late November of 1864, we see Daniel's attitude change. The food is no better than it was before, his duty is longer and more tedious if anything, but Daniel now knows for certain that his fate could be much worse, and he begins to protect the position he has gained as sentry in the Provo Yard with a small guard house to protect him from the weather. On February 2, 1865 he wrote, "If the Col. [Colonel James Lewis] gets us back to the regiment again, we need not look for much levity the remainder of our time...."

The 144th regiment was mustered into service during the late summer and early autumn of 1862 subsequent to President Lincoln's call for "300,000 more men for the suppression of the slaveholder's rebellion." It would have been more efficient and more desirable in a military sense to refill the already existing New York regiments with new recruits, thus providing for the leadership and training of the recruits by experienced officers, noncommissioned officers, and soldiers. But, it was more often the case that entire new regiments were formed with untried, but politically well-connected officers as their leaders. Such was the case with the 144th. The regimental officers learned as they trained their recruits.

When the call first came, Delaware County, New York committed to furnish a company or two to the newly formed regiment, with surrounding counties supplying the rest, but so positive was the response that nearly the entire regiment was formed with Delaware County men. They went into camp, "Camp Delaware", on the river flat near Delhi and began to drill and train in the Manual of Arms. Discipline was fairly lax, and men would sometimes leave to visit at home or with friends for a day or two. Families and friends would also visit the camp, bringing food and other comforts from home. The independent spirit of the Delaware County men was difficult for untrained, and sometimes little-respected, officers to harness.

In late September of 1862, with much flourish and many speeches, the regiment was mustered into service and marched off to war, through Hamden, Walton, Rock Rift, and finally to Hancock where they boarded a train for Washington and were put into service at the defense of that city. The regiment was engaged in various battles and skirmishes throughout the remainder of 1862 and through June of 1864 when they settled at Hilton Head as a part of the Department of the South under the command of Major General John G. Foster, a West Point trained engineer who had distinguished himself in the Mexican Wars and earlier in the Civil War.

They remained headquartered at Hilton Head until June, 1865 when the regiment moved to Elmira, New York to be mustered out of service. While headquartered at Hilton Head, much of the regiment did go off on various expeditions and fought in a number of skirmishes and small battles, but Companies D & K were left behind to perform guard duty.

By the time Daniel enlisted in late August of 1864, the Confederacy was faltering. President Lincoln had finally found generals whose ability and determination matched the industrial might of the Northern states. The battle at Gettysburg, the "high-water mark of the Confederacy", was long past. William Tecumseh Sherman's armies were at Atlanta, and would take the city on September 2nd. In November they would begin their now famous march to the sea. General Grant, recently promoted to Lieutenant General, had command of all the Union armies and was at City Point, Virginia in direct command of the forces arrayed against General Lee at Petersburg and Richmond. The final battles were coming.

Editor's Note

Daniel White was a farmer. He was born in Delaware County, New York on March 8, 1837, the son and grandson of Scottish immigrants. With the exception of the eleven months he served in the 144th New York State Volunteer Infantry during 1864 and 1865, there is no reason to believe he ever lived anywhere else.

In August of 1864, he enlisted in the Union Army for one year. Leaving his wife of a few months in the care of her parents, he went with some of his friends to an uncertain future. Assembling at Norwich, New York, the men were sent to a distribution point near New York City where they boarded a troop ship for City Point, Virginia. From there Daniel was sent by a round-about route to Hilton Head, South Carolina, where he remained, with one brief exception, until his regiment was mustered out of service in June of 1865.

Throughout his service Daniel, like most literate soldiers of his time, wrote a multitude of letters. Most of those letters were destroyed, but his wife, Amanda, saved the ones she received from him, and stored them away in a trunk. The contents of the trunk were discovered in 1972 or 1973 by my parents, while they were helping a relative dispose of the furnishings in her home in Downsville.

I recently came across the letters, and began the tedious job of transcribing them. The majority are written on 10"x 8" sheets of paper, folded in half to make a four page 5"x 8" booklet. Some of the booklets have lines, some do not. The paper is mostly of very high quality, attested to by its hundred year survival. Daniel wrote with pen and ink when he could, and the vast majority of his words are legible, though in some cases I've been unable to understand his meaning. Where words or phrases were impossible to decipher, I've tried to write each letter of the word by comparing its shape with individual letters in other words I did understand.

The most difficult problem with transcribing Daniel's letters was his style of writing. He used no paragraphs and no sentences. Each booklet is filled with one long run-on group of words. I've punctuated the letters into readable phrases, sentences, and paragraphs, but I've left much of his spelling and grammar alone. In some cases, where a word was consistently misspelled or where a misspelling detracts from the flow of the story, I've corrected it. The spelling of proper names has also been corrected. Where words or phrases don't appear to fit, or where additional clarification was needed, I've used brackets.

While transcribing his letters, I was continually surprised by Daniel's vocabulary. It seems obvious that he was better educated than others of his time and place in society. Even his brothers, through their letters to him after the war, did not display his command of language. Daniel had his linguistic eccentricities; there were some often-used words he just couldn't seem to spell correctly, and his grammar was never consistent. But, in the main, Daniel proved himself to be of above average ability when compared with those around him.

We can not be sure if all of his letters to Amanda survived. After studying them, I don't think we have a complete record. I would guess there are three, or perhaps four, missing. Maybe they were lost in transit or destroyed. Whatever the case, I have included all of Daniel's letters that are in our possession.

I have included a few letters that I think add new dimensions to his story. Two of these were letters Daniel wrote to Amanda's brother, Charles Merritt. They are included because I believe they reveal a side of Daniel's character that he did not choose to expose to his wife, at least during that early stage of their marriage. Another is a letter Amanda wrote to Daniel in June of 1865 after he had been home on furlough. It is a wonder that letter survived. Daniel must have carried it with him on his long journey home from Hilton Head.

To set the stage for the main body of his story, I have included six letters that were written before Daniel joined the 144th. Two of them he wrote to Amanda before they were married. The other four were written to Daniel by William Ruswell Stevens during 1862 & 1863. Ruswell was one of the original members of the 144th New York State Volunteers, and rose through the ranks to First Sergeant. His letters may have had some influence over Daniel's decision to join the regiment.

One other letter may appear to be unrelated to the rest of the collection. It was written by James Nichol in early November of 1864, and is addressed to Seth Conklin, a member, along with Daniel, of Company K of the 144th. Seth and Daniel were friends, and in 1878 would become brothers-in-law, when Seth married Amanda's younger sister, Anna. James Nichol was a friend also, in fact a number of references are made to his family in Daniel's letters. James served with one of the many other regiments New York State furnished to the Union. It is important to this collection because of Daniel's friendship with both Seth and James, and because Daniel would later write to Amanda about James' participation at Petersburg.

This collection of letters should not be viewed as a complete or even necessarily accurate account of the regiment's activities during 1864 and 1865. Indeed, some of Daniel's statements are not supported by historical fact, most probably because, in his words, "things are easily reported in camp." However, Daniel White's letters do provide us with an intimate insight into a short period in the life of a pretty average man, a peaceful dairy farmer whose life was interrupted by the Civil War.

Jack C. Davis
Louisville, KY
January, 1992

CHAPTER ONE

DEAR FRIEND

Miss Amanda Merritt
Downsville, Delaware County, NY

Hamden, NY
April 28, 1861

Dear Friend,

 I take the liberty to write a few lines to you, and I hope that you will excuse me. I have waited patiently a long time for you to make that long promised visit, and I have given up all hopes of seeing you and George [Merritt; Amanda's older brother] up here. He told me that he was coming home in three or four weeks, and then he was coming up, and he said that he would give you an invite to come with him, but four and five weeks have passed since then, and I have not seen either of you yet.

DEAR WIFE

I presume that you are aware of the fact that I have been in your hollow, but I did not see any of the young folks as they were all absent. However, I had a good visit.

You was cutting on me pretty hard the last time I saw you, but I think that it is my turn now. As the story goes, you are going to get married pretty shortly, and I sincerely hope that you may receive this letter before you are married as I do not relish the idea of writing to any man's wife, and if such a thing should happen, I hope you will pardon my presumption in writing to you, but if you will condecend to answer this and inform me when I may see you at home, I will come over and make one social visit, and if you know when George will be home, please write and let me know as I want to see him once more before he leaves for good, if he has not already done so, and if he comes up so you and he can come up, do not be bashful as we will be glad to see you.

I come home every Saturday night and stay until Monday morning. I should think that George would be afraid of the women after getting cracked on the head as he was a week or two ago.

I am thinking about going to war. Now days there is a number going from Town, and I have thought some of vollenteering. There is two or three drafted so they say, but the most are vollenteers that are going from Hamden. I presume that there is some drafted in your town [Colchester].

DEAR FRIEND

I have some hopes of the war producing a compromise, and I hope that it may be compromised if it can be satisfactorily and if the present difficulties are not settled. The longest winded horse holds out the longest; so it will be in this case. The party that has the most funds and the most men must conquer in the end. Ruffians make laws and fools enforce them in many cases.

I think that you will not find anything very interesting in this letter, and as I have no news to write, I shall close at present. You must excuse mistakes and there is about a peck of them here. Write as soon as convenient, and let me know how you are getting along, that is if you feel so disposed, and if you do not it is your priviledged right to do the other thing. Just put a part of this letter down as gass if you please.

From your sincere friend,
D.B. White

Tis my pen is poor,
My ink is black,
And if you cannot read this,
Send it back.

DEAR WIFE

Daniel B. White
Hamden, Delaware County, NY

                        Camp near Cloud's Mills, VA
                                    March 7, 1862

Friend Daniel,

    Without further delay I seat myself to answer your thrice welcome letter which I received last night, and as a matter of course was pleased to hear from you and to hear that you was well and enjoying yourself as well.

    I thank you very kindly for your willingness to assist me in the Morrison Company, but I think I shall not write to her as I am not any acquainted with her, and you know correspondence should be somewhat acquainted at best. You thought that I heard from some of the girls personally. I beg to inform you that I have not heard from a single person in that clove, only you, and I have written several letters to Christie's folks too, but they have not answered or have not reached them or something is the matter. Give them my kindest regards, and tell them I should be pleased to hear from them at any time.

    I like soldiering very well, and with the crisis as it is I would not come home on any consideration. But, if the war was done and the object accomplished for which I could, then I would like to go home and enjoy the liberty that our fore fathers purchased for us with a price no less than their blood.

Dan, I want to give you a little advice. Don't you never enlist unless you feel it's your duty, and if you feel that duty calls you to your Country's Service, let that call be obeyed and you will never be sorry, I assure you. Don't wait for a Draft if you have a chance to volunteer, for voluntary is the best by far. I look back on the time that I enlisted with pleasure and not regret, and I wish every one was the same. There would be less skedaddling and more good soldiers.

The health of our regiment is good at present. The boys are more contented than they were 2 months ago, and everything goes off pleasantly. We have just received intelligence that Vicksburg is taken, and it came from a reliable source, and that brightens the faces of some that are homesick and love sick and every other kind of sick.

Now Dan, you must write as often as you can, and I will do the same. Give my best respects to James [White: Daniel's brother] and his wife.

Yours truly,
W. R. Stevens
Sustain the right forever
144th Regt. NYS Vols.

DEAR WIFE

===

Miss Amanda Merritt
Downsville, Delaware County, NY

      Farmerville, Seneca County, NY
          December 27, 1862

Dear Friend,

  I now take the present opurtunity to write a few lines to you to inform you that I am well at present, and I sincerely hope that this letter will find you enjoying the same blessing.

  I started from home a week ago yesterday. I left Delaware last Thursday and took the cars [train] at Deposit and came to Ithaca that night. We then took a stage to Farmerville which is about twenty miles north of Ithaca, and we are staying at Dr. White's today. We are going to stay here until Monday. We will then go to Seneca Lake and take a steam boat to Jefferson and then take the cars to Elmira, then to West Cameron where William [Daniel's brother] lives. My cousin, John White, came with me, and Dr. White is my cousin.

  This is a very pretty village, and in view of Cayuga Lake. I cannot tell you much news as I am not acquainted with the surroundings of this place. There is two or more Brick Buildings in the place, a Baptist Church and a Blacksmith's shop &c.

DEAR FRIEND

We had a splendid ride on the cars, but confound them old stage coaches, they are enough to make one think swear unless they are Christians. I wish you could have been along when we were on the NY and Erie railroad. You would have enjoyed a ride on that I am shure.

I have not found a woman yet, and I am afraid I am so hard to suit that my chances will be pretty slim. I am coming back to Delaware some day before long if I do not run off the track.

I suppose your sleighriding would come out pretty slim Christmas. Perhaps you will make it all up New Years. I hope so at least. I should like to hear from you, but I cannot tell you where to write a letter to so I could get it, and if ever I get settled long enough in one place to hear from Delaware, I shall write to Margaret [Daniel's younger sister] and you again, but I presume I will be home before long. You can tell Margaret that if I was there I would chop her some wood. If she is as near out as she was when I came from there last it may be some consolation to her.

I shall have to close this would be letter. You must excuse mistakes as they have been raising [razzing?] me here since I commenced writing.

D.B. White

DEAR WIFE

===

Daniel B. White
Hamden, Delaware County, NY

Camp Bliss
January 8, 1863

Friend Daniel,

After an absense of some 4 months, I attempt to drop a few lines to you to let you know that I am still alive and well. You must not think by my long silence that I have forgotten you or thought of such a thing, for it wants something more than the mere separation of 4 months to destroy the recollections of friends and especially those in whom I had placed such explicit trust and confidence as I ever have in you. I should have written before, but obsticles have been constantly thrown in my way (as you know, reverses are quite prevelant in war), and I have resolved not to delay writing longer.

The health of the regiment is soon to be improving, and is alrcady much better than it has been for some time. I am well at present and have been all the time since I came here. One of my tentmates is sick now. Signor (John) is his name.

You have probably heard of the bloodless battle that the 144th had at Annandale, and I suppose you have heard of their retreat back to camp, but as it happened we did not find any rebels there to fight, so we could not fight them, but you better believe that they showed what they would do if it were: fire thick, die in half an hour. After the long roll was beaten they were in readiness, and in ten minutes more they were on the way to the place where we were ordered. We reached the place of our destination about 4 o'clock in the morning, and were drawn up in line of battle and averted an attack until the next night at dark when we were alerted to return to camp and sent further orders.

The 144th was drawn up in front with the 148th on the left of us and our right wing being supported by the 9th Mass. Battery which belongs to our Brigade and the 127th being held as a reserve in case they were needed to strengthen any part of our front that might be too weak to repel the force that might be brought against us. The 12th NY Cavelry, about 300 or 500 strong, were deployed as skirmishers, and they were situated so as to fall back and reinforce us on our right. We had a splendid position, and could, if fairly attacked, have whipped 10 to our 1 easy, but I must close as I am sleepy and must go to bed. Good night.

W.R. Stevens

Daniel, write soon. Give my respects to all the Clove folks.

DEAR WIFE

===

Daniel B. White
Hamden, Delaware County, NY

                        Post Hospital, Folly Island, SC
                                    September 6, 1863

Friend Daniel,

You no doubt begin to think that you have ceased to be remembered by me, for which you have good reason, but alow me to inform you that still you share a warm place in the heart of an absent friend. I have forgotten when I received your last letter, but think it was when we were going up the peninsula. I should have answered you sooner, but circumstances which I could not govern have caused my delay in responding to you.

I will not attempt to give you a detail of the particulars of our mankilling campaign, but suffice it to say we were gone from Yorktown just one month to a day, and from there we went to Fredrick City and thence almost to Hagerstown through Md. and then back to Berlin, between Harper's Ferry and the Point of Luck on the Potomac, where we crossed back upon the Sacred Blood Stained soil of the war, and from there we came to Charleston, SC, not staying in one place over 4 days at any time from the time we started up the peninsula until we got here. So you can judge something of the condition of the 144th. By this time they only muster about 200 men fit for duty. They have been on Morris Island 14 days since they came here.

I am sorry to say I have not been with the regiment since we landed here the 12th of August. I was sun struck in Va., but done duty all the time until we came here. I am getting better now so that I try to nurce a little, but I am very weak yet. There are also a number of others here from our regiment who are very sick, but one in particular, John George, a member of Co. E. In all human probability ere this reaches you, he will be sleeping his last long sleep from which none ever wake to weep, but still he may get well. He is a noble, brave, generous hearted fellow, and has won the well wishes of all with whom he has become acquainted, but the hand of disease shows us plainly that God plants his flowers when he thinks time and plucks at any age. Oh, why should we reprive when they as called off the stage. I hope and trust that through the will of God that he, with all the rest of us, may still be speard, but if it is to be otherwise, may we be prepared to say: "Thy will God, not mine, be done."

Trusting in him alone who has thus far sustained me, and upon whose promise we may rely, I bid you good night, knowing that those who put their trust in God He will not forsake. Write soon. I remain as ever, Yours truly.

W.R. Stevens

DEAR WIFE

Daniel B. White
Hamden, Delaware County, NY

                                        Folly Island, SC
                                        October 30, 1863

Friend Daniel,

With pleasure I acknowledge the receipt of your interesting note which I received the 25th, and this is the first opportunity I attempt to respond according to agreements. I am happy to inform you that my health is some better than when I last wrote to you, but I am not wholy recovered yet, but still I am so as to be around, and on duty part of the time, but still I don't feel as I used to before I was sick.

You spoke of the Draft. Well now Dan, I think the Draft was good enough as far as it went, but I fear if the Salvation of our Country depended on Del. Co. Conscripts and Officers, it would be eternally lost, but thank God there were Loyal hearts among the hills of Delaware who at the first 2 and 3 calls went to defend the noble rights which were purchased for us with a price no less than the Blood of our Forefathers. Shall we shrink from duty while the oppressors seek to destroy all that is Dearest to every loyal citizen. For me, I answer louder than our Bleeding country is calling in her hour of peril, "No, not while one dollar or one man is left to fight." May God speed the time when right shall rule and when the side of truth triumph over red-handed treason. I was glad to hear that the draft did not hit you, for I am sure you would not enjoy soldiering much, and then it is better for loyal men to stay than copperheads.

There is quite an excitement in camp at present in consequence of the regiment being consolidated, which I suppose will be done soon. The officers, which only one year ago swore before God and man to support the Government and Constitution, and now in the trying time, because they have the power, they resign and go home regardless of those who they, through their influence enticed to enlist and leave all that was dear to them, and then because they got shoulder straps on, they say they are no longer under obligation to those of inferior rank, and consequently they go home, and laugh in their sleeves about how nice they have got out of it. But, thank fortune it was not through the influence of any Office Seekers that I enlisted, but from a mere sense of duty, and consequently I have nothing to regret.

You must write as often as you can and tell me all the news you can hear of, for I have nothing to cheer me here except the honest conviction that I am answering the call of duty which revolves upon every loyal citizen, and he who withdraws from the duty is no longer subject to the protection of our natural laws. Let us go on then in the strength of Him who led captivity captive while we shall place the iron heel of justice upon the neck of the Traitor who dares to intrude

DEAR WIFE

upon the sacredness of our laws. And, may He who holds the destinies of nations as well as individuals in his hands soon bestow upon us as a Nation the inestimable blessing of a permanent peace.

Excuse all mistakes and bad composition and receive this,

From your ever true friend,
Wm R. Stevens

P.S. Please direct to me as I sign my name as there are others of the same name in the regiment

Wm R. Stevens
Co. K, 144th NYSV
Washington, DC

DEAR FRIEND

During this period Daniel, in his early twenties, was a farm laborer. The 1855 census lists him as working on Harrison Terry's farm in the Town of Hamden. Daniel's father, Robert White, had died in an accident while building a barn in 1846, and it appears that Daniel's oldest brother, John, took over the farm for a time, caring for the rest of the family. By 1860 Daniel's mother, Mary, and his young sister, Margaret, were living in a log house quite near Daniel's brother, James, a successful farmer in Gregory Hollow, Town of Hamden, who is often mentioned in subsequent letters. William, another brother, had moved to West Cameron, New York, some distance away from the rest of the family.

Amanda, born in 1841, lived with her parents, John and Susanna Merritt, on their farm in Huntley Hollow, Town of Colchester. She was the third of eight children.

Though Daniel and Amanda lived in different townships, the distances were not great. The village of Downsville would have been the focal point of their meetings, although in those days it was common to "make a visit" that might last days or even weeks. We can only imagine that George Merritt's friendship with Daniel may have provided the spark that eventually brought Daniel and Amanda together.

William Ruswell Stevens was 21 years old and living on his family's farm near Downsville when he joined the 144th NYSV at its inception in September of 1862. He advanced through the ranks, and was promoted to First Sergeant on April 1, 1865. He was discharged with the regiment, and in 1903 was living in Norwich, New York.

On October 24, 1863, Colonel David E. Gregory resigned his commission as Commander of the regiment, precipitating the consolidation Stevens wrote about on October 30th.

CHAPTER TWO

I Am A Soldier Now

Mrs. Daniel B. White
Downsville, Delaware County, NY

Norwich, NY
Sep. 6, 1864

Dear & Dearest Wife

It is with pleasure that I sit down to write a few lines to you. I am a soldier now and Uncle Sam clothed me yesterday. I staid in the barricks last night, slept on the hard side of a hemlock board, and it was hard indeed, but I will soon call our bed that we get here first rate. We have good bread as I wish to eat, good beef and coffee for breakfast & supper, and water, but we miss the Delaware butter. The boys call for it but it does not come, and if we get as good for the next twelve months, I shall not grumble. I tell you Amanda there is some bully boys here. They all say if the boys that are here now do not fight it out it will never be fought out. Oh Amanda, how I should like to see you this morning, but I'll bet one year from now if it should please God to spare our lives, we will hope to meet again and under the government of the United States with the flag of our Union floating on evry breeze.

The next thing that I find is the habbit of swearing. The boys seem as if they were all let loose, and it disgusts me so that I have not felt like swearing since I came in here. And mean talk, too mean to speak when alone to say nuthing of being in such a crowd as this. You must write to me as soon as I can tell you where to write. I expect to leave here tomorrow for Hart Island.

I received my bounty all right as soon as I told them what there would be for about it. My bonds are to be left in the First National Bank of Delhi for $800.00 Dolls to be deposited there by Dr. Calhoun of Bovina [Town of Bovina Enlistment Committee Member] to my order, and I have an order from him to that effect.

The Board alowed me $5.00 Dolls for my ride and 4.60 for board. I sent home $66.00 Dolls with James, and he is to let you have it after paying Thomas Williams & Alexander Shaw what they have against me. Use what you want and take care of the rest. I have some $35 Dolls with me yet, and if I get a chance I will send some more home. I will mail this today if I can. There is some risk in carying much money here, and I can get some from home if I need it.

I am glad John got clear, but should like to have him with us too. My love to all your folks & mine, for I consider yours and mine all the same.

I remain your truest friend,
D.B.White

P.S. I will tell you all about why I did not get a furlough, and evry thing else you wish to know.

Mrs. Daniel B. White
Downsville, Delaware County, NY

City Point, VA
Tuesday, Sep. 13, 1864

Dear Wife,

We are at General Grant's headquarters, lying on the sod waiting to see what they are going to do with us. Some say one thing, and some another. We are within 8 miles of Petersburg and 13 of Richmond. Maybe we will have to travel to the front. If not, we will be sent back to Fortress Monroe and round Cape Hatteras to Hilton Head.

After we left Norwich we went to New York City to the barricks at Castle Garden. The next day we went to Hart Island, staid all night there, and next day we were paid of our United States bounty, $33.33 cts., then part of us were put aboard of a transport and sent to City Point. We went aboard Saturday afternoon and just came off to day about 10 o'clock. Since then some of the men that came on the ship have been sorted out and sent to some good place I presume.

There was about 900 men on board, and the man was lucky that got a chance to sit down to say nothing about lying down. Some laid out on deck, and it rained, sometimes pretty hard. Lots of them were sea sick and gagging and spewing and other things too.

I want you to tell all your folks not to sell a farm to go as a soldier for it don't pay. Atend to Charley; $1000 is nuthing. We have seen hard times already, and expect to see worse yet, but if we get to the regiment, we hope to see better regulations.

There is about half the 144th left behind. I do not know where they are. We were all called out, and some 200 of us were taken, and the rest were left. Ed White, Clark Landfield and a lot of the Colchester boys are here. We are all split up; perhaps the rest are on the way.

I could tell you lots of things you never thought of and could not apreciate unless you saw them. A soldier's life is not to be desired, yet the boys are all pretty well, and all seem to enjoy themselves first rate. They seem to feel good, if hard used.

I just drop this to let you know how I am and where I have been. Well all the time yet. Yours truly,

D.B. White

Perhaps I shall write soon again, as soon as I can. I must close. I should be pleased to hear from you & all again.

Mrs. Daniel B. White
Downsville, Delaware County, NY

Camp Distribution, Alexandria, VA
Thursday, Sep. 15, 1864

Dear and Beloved Wife,

I take the present opportunity to write a few lines to you to let you know where I am. I started to New York a week ago last Wednesday, Thursday went to Hart Island, Friday started for City Point, reached there Monday night, staid all night on the transport, went next day to show ourselves to General Grant, staid all day round there until near night, put on board another boat for Alexandria, arived there this morning. So, you see I have had quite a water tour.

I wrote to Antoinette [White: cousin, also refered to as Nett or Net] and described things partly, but you cannot comprehend our situation unless you saw it. If any party ever was srached round as we have, I should like to see them, but we are all soldiers, so who cares.

We expect to go to Hilton Head soon. We do not know when, perhaps in ten minutes and perhaps not in two weeks. We have not known when or where since we left Norwich. The boys that were left behind at Hart Island have not come up yet. We expect them tonight. The most of the boys that are with me are mostly Colchester boys. Billy Johnston is with us.

We are 3½ miles from Alexandria, and within 5 or 6 miles of Washington. We saw the capitol this morning as we marched up to Camp Distribution, I think on Arlington Heights. We have passed Fortress Monroe twice, and will have to go back there to start for Hilton Head. They are riding us round on pleasure trips to see the country, and feed us on hard tack, and let the petty officers cheat us out of our rations.

We all feel pretty good. If you saw us you would think we never saw hard times. You would not believe how my feelings have changed since I was a soldier. I should not care if they put me anywhere that the rest of the boys went, if it was in the front. I think that it puts fight in a man pretty quick to be in the army. I still think that I can live one year in the army, and if I do there will be one good feeling fellow as you ever saw in your life.

Oh, how much I would give to go home and stay jist one night. I want you to think of me morning, noon, and night, just as you would about the best friend you ever had, and be shure that I will never forget my love for you as long as ever I think of anything.

I have tried this afternoon to get my photograph to send home, but could not as there was so many ahead, but if I stay here tomorrow, I shall try to get it, and perhaps I cannot get but one and you will have to have some taken from it. I want Esther [White: James' wife] to have one, and Magie [Margaret White] one, Mother one, and Nelly [Ellen Nichol: Daniel's sister] one, and the most of your folks one. I want you to get yours taken, and send it to me as soon as I can have a chance to stay in one place long enough to get it sent to me. Get a photograph and I will run the risk of getting a case here, as you could not send it verry well another way. I should like to have Antoinette's too, if I could get it, and all the rest of my friends, but I suppose that will be impossible.

I AM A SOLDIER NOW

I cannot write all I want to on one sheet, and fill it all up at that, but I shall write often.

I told James to give you some money after paying my debts, amount about $10.00 dollars. I sent, I think, $66. dolls home with him. I sent an order for James to draw my bonds as I thought he could attend to it as well as any one, and as convenient. You must tell him to take out his expenses going to Norwich, then take what money you want. I presume I have written all this before, as I have forgotten half I wrote before. I shall write to my friends as soon as I can get time.

Yours ever and truly,
D.B. White

My love to all and you too.

We have fine quarters here, and I should like to stay here one year if they use us as well as at present. The nearer headquarters, the better used.

DEAR WIFE

Mrs. Daniel B. White
Downsville, Delaware County, NY

                    Camp Distribution, Alexandria, VA
                                  Friday, Sep. 16, 1864

Dear Wife,

    I catch the present opurtunity to write a few lines this morning. I had my Ambrotype taken this morning, and shall send it on as soon as I can get round. I had to stand three times, and do not think it first best yet, but I send it to be there. I shall send some photographs as soon as I can. We have to wait three days for them, and I do not know that I shall be here as long as that.

    We have a very pleasant place here, too pleasant to last long. We will have to try the water soon again. We will have to ride 1,500 [miles] yet to get to our regiment. We have been on the water 5 days and nights already. We all feel good. That is a soldier's life, one day all right, the next day all wrong. Just as it happens Hart Island was the toughest place we have found yet. Just speak of Hart Island, and you would hear the boys begin to swear, and some of them are good at it too.

    The rest of the boys have not come here yet. At Hart Island we had nothing to eat but dry bread, and every petty officer would misuse us to boot, but we are where a man is a man here.

The country looks different from what I supposed it would. You would think that there never was any thing but a barren country, no fences, no houses scarcely, and what there is is about as good as your folkses barn. The country is all covered with brush of one kind and another, mostly scrubby pine.

Tell Jane Conklin I send my respects to her and her folks, and should write to them as soon as I can, but tell all that enquire after me that I have not forgotten them, and if they were here they would see things in the way they would not think of till they tried it, to hinder writing.

You must let me know whether you can read this pencil writing after it is carried, as it is much harder to write with a pencil than with a pen. There is less or more bustle here all the time. You will not look for Gentry letters from me, it takes up the room I can get, and always falls short with me. I would write news to you all day, and then see a great deal more to say yet.

You must feel good and enjoy yourself as good as you can. Go a visiting one day, and somewhere next.

DEAR WIFE

Tell Carrie [Hitt] when you write to her that I send my respects to her and her folks. I guess I shall have to write to them soon again.

You was disappointed perhaps that I did not go home from Norwich, but I could not see how it was going to make things any better to leave again than it was when I did, and I should have been behind the rest of the boys all the time, and [that] would not have been very pleasant for me. It took us all to take care of our things, and then some of them had their things stole. I would liked to have gone home as well as you would like to see us.

My respects to all, and yours ever,
D.B. White

Mrs. Daniel B. White
Downsville, Delaware County, NY

Hilton Head, SC
Wednesday, Sep. 28, 1864

Dear Wife,

Here we are at Hilton Head, Co. K, 144th Regiment. We got here last night, all alive, but not all well. Billie McDonald has been pretty hard up for 4 or 5 days, but is better this morning. Charles Bogart is rather off the hooks and James Radeker, but they are all feeling better this morning. I have been pretty well all the time.

We all had a hard time coming from Camp Distribution. We started with five days rations in our harver sacks, and some was short. We had hard tack and a piece of fat pork, raw. The water that was put on board for us was as bad as any you have seen in that barrel at the back door this summer. It stunk so we could not smell it, let alone drink it, and it was full of wiglers, so it had to be strained to get rid of them. Some of the boys bought water at $1.00 for a canteen and 50¢ for a cupful, and the boys that were sick had to have what we could get. I tell you that riding on those transports is no better than it is called.

I have seen J.D. Scott, G. Barber, F. Stewart, Rufus Conklin and Seth [Conklin] and lots of others, but the regiment is all split up, and some is here and some across the river and somewhere else. They have called out some of the company and taken part and left some. I think that they will be transferred into other companies, and after the regiment is full they will be put into other regiments. Our Company has not been called on yet, and I do not know where I will be put; Co. C took 25 and left the rest.

DEAR WIFE

Afternoon

It is just as I expected. Co. K has been called, and 37 men taken and the rest put in other companies. I have been put in Co. K, if there is no gouge game played between now and night. Curt and John Bradley were transferred, after they were in the company, by the influence of some of the boys that were here. Some have bought their chances, and paid as high as $15.00 for the change.

The weather is verry warm here. We all suffer of heat. The water is middling good.

The chance for the boys that went home on furlough is pretty slim to get in the 144th. Some of them will have to go in other regiments. I am going to try to get in the Engineer Corps. Our orderly says there will be a chance for some of the boys, and he will do about right with me if there is any chance.

Some of the Engineers is going home. If I can get there, I will be all right, but I do not build my hopes verry high on that yet.

I will write soon again. You must write me as soon as you can, and tell evrybody to write to me.

Direct to: Hilton Head, SC
             Co. K, 144 Regt. NYSV
Your friend, ever the same in SC or in old Delaware.
D.B. White

I AM A SOLDIER NOW

═══════════════

Mrs. Daniel B. White
Downsville, Delaware County, NY

> Hilton Head, SC
> Monday, Oct. 3, 1864

Dear Wife,

I am well at present, and I hope these lines may find you all the same. We are getting things shaped so we are more comfortable now than we were. We have our tent in a shape that we live in it. Buell Robinson, Corneal Bennett, & Shaver Gunn [Adam S. Gunn] tent with me. Our duty is the same as when I wrote before. We get up at 5, answer to 5 roll calls: three calls for meals, two for drill. We drill 4 hours each day. We get whiskey once a day if we want it. I have drawn three rations since I came here. It is mostly quinine and water. The old soldiers recommend us to take our rations as it helps to keep fever & ague away. George Barber has the fever & ague once in a while. He had the shaking last week once. It left him pretty weak for a few days. He sends his respects to you all.

We had a little frace [fracas ?] with Buell Friday night. They commenced talking politics, and Buell was pretty fast. Him and Dan Smith had the most to say. Smith is a Lincoln man, and I find the most of the boys that were here is Lincoln men. Buell alowed that any man that supported the present administration and voted for Abe Lincoln this fall was a traitor to his country. After roll call Buell came to the tent and took off his clothes and went to bed. The boys thought they would have a little fun with him so they appointed Conrad Disco to take him. He put on his straps and came to the tent & asked if Buell was there. I told him he was. Well, he said, he supposed he would have to take him to the gard house. Buell wanted to know who it was that was going to take him and by who's order and what for. Conrad said he was a gard and was going to take him by order of the Officer of the Day and if he could get him off he would, but he must go with him. Buell got up and dressed and started. Conrad took him down to the cook house and told him to stand there till he went and seen the Captain. When he came back he told Buell if he would promise not to talk any more sesesh he might go to his quarters. Buell was tickled enough to get the priveledge to go to his tent. I do not know whether he has found out the game that was played on him yet or not, but the boys declare if he talks so again they will take him in earnest yet, as he violated his oath talking as he did that night.

We had Army Regulations read to us today. They are strict enough, I tell you.

I shall not write any more today to you. I have written a letter for H. Tiffany [Henry] & one to Bill Johnston. I shall write to you soon again. I shall be on duty tomorrow or next day. The boys that we left at Norwich has not arived here yet, and those that went home on furloughs will not get in the regiment. That is one reason I did not take a furlough. Some of the boys received letters last night. I have not got any yet. Ed White got one last night. The mail goes from here once a week.

From your friend
D.B. White

Direct to   Daniel B. White
Co. K, 144th Regt.
Hilton Head, SC

Mrs. Daniel B. White
Downsville, Delaware County, NY

> Hilton Head, SC
> Sunday, Oct. 9, 1864

Dear Wife,

With pleasure I catch the present opurtunity to pen a few lines to an ever faithful friend. I have been healthy since I started from home with a verry few exceptions. I was off duty day before yesterday, but I came round all right again and feel like a soldier today again.

We have business enough to atend to each day. If any person thinks that soldiers have nuthing to do, tell them to come and try get up at 5 in the morning, atend to roll call 3 times, drill 4 hours and dress parade which takes an hour, then take your turn at fatigue and cleaning our Avenue, black your boots, brighten your buttons on your coat, number 16, buttons on our cap, brass plates on our belt and cartridge box, then keep our gun so bright that we can see our face if we keep them right. It takes me one solid hour evry morning and ½ hour at night. So you may calculate about how much time we have to ourselves after atending to our meals and other nesessary duties. [I am] buying sugar for I cannot make any rations last me. Then tobacco, I think I can chew as much as any should, whether in the army or at home. If I get back I will show you how I do it.

We drew dress coats and guns yesterday. We have to atend Company Inspection evry Sunday, and I presume oftener. Shortly, for Company Inspection, we have to have our knapsacks all packed, woolen blanket, rubber blanket packed in just such a shape, our clothes all in order and in our knapsacks, overcoat rolled after a style which they have in the army and strapped on the top of our knapsacks. Then evry day we have to have our tents sweeped and our clothes all hung up, our blankets aired.

I AM A SOLDIER NOW

Politics is up to par here at present. We will all have a chance to vote this week. I think shall hardly take the trouble to vote this fall. I find the politics in the regiment very different from what I supposed. Some used to preach at home that all our old soldiers were Demicrats, and if they went from home Republicans they would turn before they were in the army a year. I find perhaps two in our company that will support McClellan, and I think I alow more for him than he will get. There is some recruits that will vote for McClellan, but the majority alows that his platform is not the thing for these times. I do not like Lincoln, and therefore I am indifferent about voting.

Those old soldiers are bitter against Little Mc.. George Barber alows that Orbin will vote for Mac, but he alows that he would like to be where he could just give him one of his boots in his hinder. He thinks that he could give Hannah a job to act as hospital nurse. Hiram Gray is just there too. They all alow that there is men that they would rather have than Old Abe, but they cannot see it this fall.

We have good news from Sheridan and Grant, and I hope that we will see peace and happiness in our land once more and speedily too.

I enjoy myself very well here, but I cannot bare to contrast it with home and home enjoyments. You know how that is as well as I can tell you.

Now, the sick. Bill McDonald does not get round verry fast altho he is not danjerous. I think Charley Bogart has the measles. It is a bad place to have them. There is no chance to keep any person warm when it is chilly.

Last night was colder than it has been since we came here. It was comfortable with a woolen blanket and rubber [blanket] over us. I think it was not so cold, but we felt it, the weather being so warm previous to this time.

Charles Elmore was taken severely with some fever, but he is some better to day.

I think it is time for me to stop writing for the present. The band came last Monday, and about 300 men. The regiment was filled, then the remainder are consigned to the Engineer Corps. Some have been taken out of our company and consigned to the Engineer Corps.

I want you to see or send word to Margaret and Dan [Frasier] that I send my best respects to them. I shall write to them as soon as I can. I have written to John Conklin last week and Robert Christie and Net White. I have not received any letters from home yet. The mail boat is due today. I shall be disappointed if I get none when the mail arives. The mail leaves here and comes here once a week.

I think of nuthing more at present. Give my respects to all, and I remain as ever your true friend.

I AM A SOLDIER NOW

D.B. White

With love and hope for home and friends so kind.

━━━━━━━━━━

Mrs. Daniel B. White
Downsville, Delaware County, NY

Hilton Head, SC
Tuesday, Oct. 11, 1864

Dear Wife,

It is with pleasure that I seat myself to inform you that I feel like a skunk this morning, but I look like a soldier of the Uncle Sam style, just like my comrades as near as I can.

I acknowledge the receipt of two letters from you. I received them this morning. Altho there was bad news, it makes me feel fifty per cent better to hear from home and you. I feel that it is bad news to hear from John being so sick. How I should like to see him. I shall feel anxious until the mail arives again. That will be about a week. Tell him to take courage and try hard to get better. Tell him I am coming home in about one year, God willing. And, I feel willing to submit to his wise decree knowing that his ways are not like our ways, but He doeth all things well. May He protect you all; the same with me.

You felt that City Point letter was a damper. I know nuthing of the contents of that letter. I cannot remember anything scarcely that I have written to anyone. I think that this will be the 24th letter that I have written since I left home, and I never think of what I have written after I finish a letter. If you had went through the mill that we all had just at that time, taken right up almost to the front, knowing nuthing about where we should have to go, evrybody surmising trouble, perhaps you would have been as down as I was at the heel.

You wanted me to inform you about the amount of money I sent home with James. As to that, I presume I was mistaken. I took no memorandum of the amount. It was an easy matter for me to be mistaken, but not so easy for James to be mistaken. You may be shure that he will give you all that belongs to you unless he has learned new tricks verry lately. I want you to tell him to take out his expenses going to Norwich as it was a great favour to me. I feel that my business is safe in his hands. And, tell him if there was a mistake, he knows about it better than I do, as my mind was on other things about that time in the day.

You done well with those lambs. You will have to write heaps of news to me when you get time, but do not rob yourself of rest to write to me at present. Write to me often, and I shall be contented with short letters until John gets better. I know that you are indifferent about your own comfort. Sometimes I think you had better take some of the advice you gave to me and take care of your own health. You must feel cheerful as I do, and I'll bet you will feel better than you do at present. What would I care for home if I could not meet you when I arived at home.

Tell your folks that I shall write to you most of the letters I write until I get more time, and I mean them all evry time, and I want them all to write to me when they can. Oh, if John and all the rest was well, how good I would feel today. My back has been a little lame since I was sick last Thursday.

James Scott wanted me to give you his respects and let him know how his Parlor Rosy gets along. I say, "Bully for 'Em".

I am sorry to hear that Frank has enlisted. He was free from Draft. I think I shall not have time to write to James this mail. If you see any of my folks, tell them that I am well and feel like a fighting cock.

I think you made yarn in a hurry. Now I want you to feel all right on my acount, and be sure that I am enjoying myself capital at present. Never look for trouble in the future, that will come soon enough.

DEAR WIFE

There is changes in the regiment and company, but I cannot find time to write about that at present (Fall-In for Drill).

You need not be alarmed about letters not reaching me. There are a verry few that do not reach their destination. The surest way to direct is Washington, D.C., but sometimes we get a letter a few days sooner to direct to Hilton Head. I think that will be the best at present until the regiment moves, then Washington, D.C. will be the best until we get settled again.

I have just come in from drill, and it is near dinner time. I will write to some of you evry mail if possible. I shall have to close for the present. I will have to write a letter today to send my vote if I vote at all, and I will have to write for Henry Tiffany.

Oh, how I should like to clasp you to my heart once more. But I love you all the same, and remain your devoted husband.

D.B. White

The weather has been chilly for a few days, but it is warmer today.

I AM A SOLDIER NOW

Mrs. Daniel B. White
Downsville, Delaware County, NY

> Hilton Head, SC
> Saturday, Oct. 15, 1864

Dear Wife,

I take a few spare moments to write a few lines to you. I have been drilling on my gun since dinner. We have no drill in the Manual of Arms, it being Saturday afternoon, and we have to fix up for Sunday inspection.

I have pretty good prospects for being detailed on picket duty tomorrow, and if I am it will throw me out of the time I generally take to do the most of my writing. I have never been on guard yet, but all the recruits are put on guard now. Some of them have taken their turn for some time, but the Major alowed that they had better drill their recruits before they detailed them on guard, but he alowed last night that most of them would pass for guard, so they commensed this morning on detail for guards, taking them as they run. It takes about 20 guards out of our company each day.

I have a letter partly written to James. I thought I should get it ready for the last mail, but I was called out before I had it finished, and consequently it had to lay over.

DEAR WIFE

I am well today, and it is my sincere hope that these lines may find you all well when this reaches you, but I look for a letter from home when the mail comes in. It is due today, but it is a chance if we get any mail here before tomorrow or next day. I am living in hopes of good news, but sometimes I am afraid of the news that is expected, but I hope for the best. The health of the regiment is improving.

I think I shall have to go out on Dress Parade in a few minutes, so I will bid you good by for the present. You must always give my respects to all my friends, and I shall write a few lines to you after the mail comes in.

Oct. 16, 1864
Afternoon Sunday,

I am well today & kicking round. The mail has not arived yet, & I am not on guard today, but I expect it evry day. I hope the mail will hurry up for I can't hardly wait.

We have had splendid weather for the last week, dry and a cool air usually.

We have had Company Inspection today. We have to take out our gun & straps & canteen, haversack, knapsack and all our nesessary accouterments with 40 rounds of cartridges. There is to be Regimental Inspection this afternoon at 4 o'clock. We still have to take out all our traps with us.

The officers come round Sunday to inspect our tents to see that evrything is kept in order and clean.

Monday, Oct. 17, 1864

I was detailed on fatigue this morning, and about 50 of us went downtown to unload the mail boat, but they were not ready so we sat round until after inspection call. We have monthly inspection today. Evrything in camp is inspected. We have busy times here. The 144th, or what of it is here, does the town duty and guard the whole island except a little help we get from a Negro regiment here.

I keep writing evry day when I can find time for I do not think that I will have time to write a verry long letter when the mail boat gets ready to leave. We will get our mail tonight or tomorrow morning. As I told you the mail boat is in the harbour, but it takes one day to get the mail overhauled & distributed. I suppose I will have to go down this afternoon to help unload her.

What we style downtown is to headquarters, about 1½ miles from camp. There is several things that pass for houses, and some are quite decent. Others are mear huts. I shall have to close for the present. It is near noon, and we will have our tents inspected. I will write more if I have time.

DEAR WIFE

Tuesday, Oct. 18, 1864

I catch a few moments more this morning. I am well and going on picket today. I received a letter last night from you, and how much pleasure it gave me to hear from home. I have received no letters from anyone else yet. Your letter was dated the 2nd.

I was glad to hear from John, but he does not gain as fast as I had hoped he would, but I hope he will get better soon. Tell George & Fatina that I will write to them as soon as I get time, and give them my respects.

You wanted to know about those old sheep. You may do as you see fit. I told Bill he might have them at $1.50, and I told Charley he might have three for $1.00. You may do the best you can, and I am satisfied.

Those watches — you take your choice. I think the one I had is worth the most. You may give the other to Margaret as soon as convenient, but do not put yourself out of the way. I fear you are indifferent about yourself. Do not tire yourself out running over that mountain.

I sent John's satchel home with George Landt to be left at Clark Andrews' Hotel. There was some clothes in it of Peter Littlejohn's. I wrote to James to get it and take charge of it.

You seem to feel disappointed about my not going home on furlough. I will give you the reason. We all calculated that the first here the first served. So it was, but if I had known how it was coming out, I should not have been in such a hurry. All that came after the regiment was filled were put into the (C) Engineer Corps. They are on the same island at present, at least some companies of the Corps. They will not let me go into the Engineer Corps. I asked the Orderly what was the reason. He said I was too good a soldier.

Wednesday, Oct. 19, 1864

I have just come from picket. I have to hurry to get this in. The mail will close soon. I had a pretty tough time yesterday. It rained all the forenoon. We stand two hours and off 4. We stand 8 hours in 24. I shall have to close for the present. I will tell you about the Engineer Corps. and several other things. We sleep on the soft side of a pitch pine slab.

Your sincere friend,
D.B.White

DEAR WIFE

Mrs. Daniel B. White
Downsville, Delaware County, NY

Hilton Head, SC
Sunday, Oct. 23, 1864

Dear Wife,

I find leasure to write a few more lines today. I am well, and I sincerely hope this may find you all enjoying the same blessing.

We got have got through with Company Inspection and inspection of quarters. The next is Regimental Inspection at 4 o'clock this afternoon.

I was permanently detailed for fatigue last Wednesday. I have to work 8 hours each day, Sunday excepted. There is 14 detailed to work on the fort breastworks & parapet, to cut down the weeds and repair the works. We think it will take two or three months, but I presume I will not be alowed to stay in that squad long. There is men that can do that duty that are not fit for night duty. We work from 7½ o'clock until 11½ o'clock, then from 1½ until 5½ o'clock. We have a good sittuation. We work just as we are a mind to. There is no fault found if we work half the time and watch the officers the other half. It gives us more time to ourselves than the boys that stand guard. They have to work at fatigue when not on guard. They call nearly all the boys out on fatigue evry day now.

I think they are coming down rough on the 144th, and we see the affects of it in camp too. There is hardly a tent that has no sick in them. At present our tent and mates have come out pretty well, but we have one sick now. Corneal Bennett was taken with the ague last Thursday and has been quite sick ever since. He thinks he is some better this morning. Billie McDonald has been taken to the hospital, also Delansie Fransisco, and there is two or three more in our company that should be there.

Our boys come down on the Captain [John Rich] and doctors last night. This morning Dr. [John] Leal alowed that Co. K had better be attended to, so I hope the sick will fare better in the future, for there is room for them to do so.

There is verry few in camp today, only the sick and those that came off guard this morning.

You mentioned in your last letter that James & Et were going to Cannonsville. I wish you could acompany them, for I am sure that they would be pleased to have you make them a visit. I forgot to write anything about it in my last letter to D. Nichol requesting them to make you a visit.

The mail has not come yet, & I presume it will not come for two or three days yet. I should like to hurry it up if possible so I could hear from John again, and you may be sure that I am pleased to hear from you all. I hope that you will not be careless enough about writing so I shall miss getting a letter each mail. I want you, or some of you, to make it a point to write once a week or I shall not grumble at twice a week.

I think Dan and Mag are shoving out [?]. I thought I should write to Dan this mail, but if they are going in on Inch Shapes [?], I am not feeling verry ambitious about writing to them.

We do not know how long we may stay here, perhaps all winter, and perhaps we may not stay here two weeks. We find it pretty cool here most of the time for the last two weeks. We are comfortably warm each day, but it is rather cool at night for our houses and bedding. I have slept with Corneal, and I have not felt verry comfortable. He has to get up nights, and that ads to our discomfiture.

I hardly know what to write that would be interesting to you. I will write some more to some of you when the mail goes out.

We have rather rough times, but nuthing to what we will have I presume. I think I shall draw another woolen blanket as soon as I can get one, if I have to throw it away in another week. I am bound to sleep warm if I can. I shall just tell them if I cannot have things about as I want them, I shall just settle with them and go home.

Henry Radecker was detailed out of our company in the Engineer Corps. They have examined them all again and thrown out several and given them their discharge. Radecker has been thrown out of the Engineer Corps., but whether he will be sent home or asigned to the Invalid Corps. we do not know yet.

I shall write no more at present. I feel as though I can stand my hand with any of the boys, but if I do not have my health, then I may feel as downhearted as any of them. I sincerely hope I may see my home and friends again with peace and prosperity reigning in our land again, but God knows best. I leave my fate in his hands after doing my duty to myself & felow men & Country.

Tuesday, Oct. 25, 1864

I take my pen in hand to write a few more lines to you. The mail has come in today, but I have received no letters from home this mail. I received a letter from John McLarren. He told me that Helen Christie was in the hollow and John was getting better. I supposed that I would shurely get a letter from home.

Buell has received no letter, nor Henry Tiffany, so I can hear nuthing direct from home. I think Jim does not put himself to much trouble to write. I have a letter to send to Net this mail & D. Frasier. Now I am going to stop writing to anyone until they see fit to answer letters that I have written.

I am well and out on fatigue today and shall be, I suppose, for some time to come.

Ruswell [Stevens] received a letter from Wes, but he writes nuthing to interest me. That draft troubles me the most now.

Colonel [James] Lewis came with the last boat. Charley Bogart, Liss Campbell, & Sam Freely have gone to the general hospital tonight. Ed White is rather poorly, but is going round all the time. George Rowe is sick, but how bad I do not know. The most of the other sick in our company is rather on the gain. Co. C came to camp yesterday. They are all well except two or three. I saw Billie Johnston. He is tough as a bear.

I must close for the present. You must be shure to write. I remain your affectionate husband,

D.B. White

I AM A SOLDIER NOW

Mrs. Daniel B. White
Downsville, Delaware County, NY

Hilton Head, SC
Thursday, Oct. 27, 1864

Dear Wife,

I have written one letter to you to go home this mail, and I thought I would write one more. If I have to do all the writing, I will just commense, yet I know verry well that you are not to blame for my not getting letters, for I am sure that you have written unless you have been in circumstances that you could not do so. Buell received a letter today that had been to Fort Pulaski, & I presume that letters get on the wrong road sometimes.

I am well and fit for duty evry day so far, & if I continue to eat my rations, I think I shall come out all right.

Jonas More is sick at present. He has had one of the government chills, but not so bad as some have them. Joan, Ed White, & Enos [More] are going to send for some things, & I thought as they asked me to, if I wanted to have anything sent, I would have you send me a pair of socks, as one pair of home made socks are worth 4 pair of government socks. I think one pair more will last me this winter. You will have a chance to see some of More's people before they send the box. You can tell them that I want room for one pair of socks, and Jonas will mention it to their folks. Perhaps there will be a chance to send a few dried berries if you have them to spare. If not, all right, I can live on Uncle Sam's rations, if I have my health. You need not send many if you any.

I will have to close for the present. I hope this will find you all well and then I am satisfied. I think you will have your match to read this, as I have written in a hurry.

I remain as ever your sincere friend and loving husband,

D.B. White

Mrs. Daniel B. White
Downsville, Delaware County, NY

Hilton Head, SC
Wednesday, Nov. 2, 1864

Dear Wife,

I seat myself to write a few more lines to you. I finished a letter to Net before dinner, and I will write to you again now. I shall not forget to write to you. I was called out on duty, and I take a few moments this evening.

I AM A SOLDIER NOW

I have heard some news since I wrote to Net. We have one more to the hospital this afternoon. His name is George Leonard. Faley Kingsley is in the regimental hospital.

There was a man died from Co. D, James Wilson from Colchester, and we have been informed of the death of Charles Bogart. He died today at 12 o'clock today. J. Wilson died last night at 12 o'clock.

I will not write any more tonight. I have no letters yet from home. The mail boat brought only 3 letters for Co. K. There is another boat that came in this afternoon. They say that our mail is on the boat. If so, we will get mail tomorrow.

I will bid you good by for tonight.

Thursday, Nov. 3, 11 o'clock

Just came in off fatigue. The corpse of J. Wilson just passed through camp, the brass band playing his funeral dirge.

Co. K received their mail this morning. One letter from J. White is all I received. No news from you yet, just when I wished the most to hear from of any place in all the world. The last letter from you was dated Oct. 2nd. I think it is strange that I do not hear from you. I will write three or four to you this mail. I will have to wait 7 or 8 days before I have a chance to get any mail.

I have heard today that it is a mistake about Charley Bogart being dead. I hope that it is true that he is alive, and I hope that he will be with us again soon. I will find out before the mail closes. He is a good boy, and we all think a great deal of him.

I do not know what to write to you. James said you would not take any money from him. Now, if you want any to use, I hope you will do so and not want for any necessarys while I am away. It is hard enough to stay at home and have the necessarys of life, I know it would be tough for me to stay there now if I had not all that is near and dear for me to stay for.

Oh, the army is the bully place where we have to be as economical as a miser to have our rations hold out, ----ed by superiors whom a great share of us would consider our inferiors at home. Our Captain told us one day that he wanted to have us salute the shoulder straps that they wore not the men that wore them. He is a pretty good fellow. I think his name is [John] Rich.

I have 5 or 6 letters written to send this mail, and I have to write two or three for Henry Tiffany, and sometimes I have to write for C. Elmore.

I AM A SOLDIER NOW

I will give you a list of the price I have to pay for some things: Butter - 75 to one dollar per pound, Onions - 15 to 25 cts. per pound, Cheese - 40 to 50 per pound, Crackers - 40 cts. per pound, Sugar - 30 to 40 cts. per pound, Tobacco - $1.50 per pound, Small Apples - 5¢ a piece, large ones - 10 or 15 Dol. per barrel, Tripoli - 15 cts. per box (and one will brighten brass for about 2 weeks), Boot Blacking - 15 cts. per box. One will last 2 - 3 weeks, but I do not use any except Sunday now, since I was detailed, or scour my gun only once a week. We have Saturday afternoon to brush up for Sunday inspection.

Whiskey you cannot buy, and I am glad of it. The whiskey that we get is one whiskey and two quinine, and any that loves whiskey can have mine as I do not draw it only once a week. They told us that it is good to keep off the chills. Perhaps it is. It should be for it is punishment enough to drink it to have some benefit from it.

I do not buy much lately, very little since I came here. It cost me enough to live to get here. I sometimes buy a few crackers when I have no bread. We get out of bread by their not drawing it regular. We draw a loaf a day, and one third is small for a meal when we get it regular. Sometimes I get a piece of cheese. If we buy a pie, we have to pay 25 or 30 cts. for it, and the crust would make good taps for your shoes. If I could get them sent home, I would have you one pair. I think they would last you one year.

DEAR WIFE

I have heard from Charley Bogart. I think it is reliable that he is alive and a little better. The other boys at the hospital are all getting along quite good.

It rains here today. A cold rain set in last night. It rained nearly all night. It stopped just in time to let us work in the forenoon. It set in again just as we came in. Fatigue, it is time to go again, but it rains at present. You may realize the position of a guard in such a storm. They have to stand their tour through thick and thin.

I am well and feel good all the time so far, only my bed does not lie as our bed in the bedroom where we used to sleep. The hard side of the slabs that I sleep on, they make my old bones ache. I have rheumatism some. I have seen a good many nights that I had to raise myself up on my hands to turn over in my bed, but it is all for the ----- . So who cares; who would not sell a farm to go as a soldier.

Buell & Tiffany did not get any mail this time.

There is very few white women on the island. There is lots of wenches, but they will barely speak to a private soldier. They alow that the officers comes in ahead. I am willing, yet I believe they tell the truth, for I think the officers take a great deal of pains, at least some of them, to have the good will of the wenches.

I AM A SOLDIER NOW

Now if I knew how you all are and how John is, I would feel better. No more at present.

Yours till death,
D.B. White

This is miserably written as you can see with half an eye.

CHAPTER THREE

IT IS A COLD WINTER IN SOUTH CAROLINA

Mrs. Daniel B. White
Downsville, Delaware County, NY

> Hilton Head, SC
> Friday, Nov. 4, 1864

Dear Wife,

    I will write a few more lines to you tonight. I have a verry poor place to write as you will see from my letter.

    I still enjoy the blessing of good health. It is cold weather for South Carolina, not cold enough to freeze yet. I suppose we feel the cold worse than we would if we were at home.

IT IS A COLD WINTER IN SOUTH CAROLINA

I have mailed one letter to you and one to Net. I think they have gone to town to start for Delaware with a boat tomorrow. I have sent only 7 letters yet this mail, so I think I will bother some of them reading them if they do not take the trouble to answer them.

We had a gay old time sleeping last night. It was so wet where Corneal & Shave sleep that they bunked with me. There was not room enough to alow us to sleep 3 abreast, so Corneal slept with his head to our feet. Shave & Corneal are on guard downtown tonight, so I have Buell for my tentmate tonight.

I wish I could have your picture. I believe it would be good for my eyesight about now. I am going to send another home before long, just as soon as I weigh about 10 pounds more. I have not gained enough yet. I want you to see if I have not improved some in soldier appearance. I would like to have Net's likeness if she would send it to me. I am going to send you a book, perhaps this mail, & a picture for you to see how troops leave New York. It is as good as life and just as I found it, only I went off one transport on another, but going in the holes is natural as life.

I have no news to write, so I will bid you good by. How I should like to step into Papa John's [Merritt] tonight and see you all. I think I could find room to warm, and it would be verry acceptable.

DEAR WIFE

Enos More received a letter from his father. He said John was so he was out round some, and your father was not verry well. Tell your folks that Old Dan White is just the old chap he always was. If he has as many bosses as he has fleas, but they will be as what used to be if it keeps as cold as it is for a few days longer. I have not heard from the hospital boys today. Give my love to all, and retain a goodly share for yourself.

From your affectionate & ever true friend,
Old Dan White the Land Pirate
Remember
me

Seth Conklin [from: James Nichol]
Co. K, 144th NYSV
Hilton Head, South Carolina

In camp near Petersburg, VA
Friday, November 4, 1864

Dear Friend Seth,

It is with great pleasure I sit down to answer your letter. I received it this morning, and was sorry to hear that you were sick. Hoping that you will get better soon.

IT IS A COLD WINTER IN SOUTH CAROLINA

We came to where the regiment was lying in camp on the 19th of September. We lay there about ten days and marched to the front, and on the 30th we were in battle with the rebels. We lay under fire a good while, and were then ordered to fall back. We fell back a little way, and then got the order, "Every man for himself", and you may believe we obeyed it too.

We lost about fifty men in our regiment, a good many taken prisoners, but I came out all sound. It is no great fun to be in a fight. We have been under fire three times since the battle, so you can see we are getting our share. I think if I was in the 144th, I could stand my year out without much danger. I think I could stand it pretty well if they would give me more hardtack and less bullets. However, I stand it well. I am as fat as a hog and as tough as a jackass.

The voting for the election is past here. In our regiment it went two hundred and fifty for Lincoln and twenty eight for McLellan. The rest of the regiments here, about the same. Old Abe must go in.

The Second and Fifth Corps, along with ours [went] on a reconaisance on the 27th of October. Our regiment was sent to a fort in our lines and part of it on picket. I was along with them. We were on post to the right of where they were fighting. We advanced about a mile, and the next day we were driven into our old post again. So much for the Johnnies.

DEAR WIFE

When we came here first we worked all night and day for a week, Sunday not excepted, building forts and breastworks.

There is some talk of our Corps going to winter at Washington or Baltimore. I hope so.

I had a letter from home yesterday, and they were all well. Your folks were well also. They said that Hannah [Conklin] was going to live with her aunt this winter.

We have got to drill four hours every day. I did not like it at first, but I like it better now. It is all quiet here now, and there is not much going on

You must write soon, and tell Rufus to write also. Send me Andrew's address.

Give my best respects to all the boys that I know. I must bid you good bye.

Yours truly,
James Nichol

IT IS A COLD WINTER IN SOUTH CAROLINA

===

Mrs. Daniel B. White
Downsville, Delaware County, NY

>Camp of the 144th
>Hilton Head, SC
>Tuesday, Nov. 8, 1864

Dear Wife,

I again take my pen in hand to the accomplishment of writing one more letter to you. I am pleased and happy to inform you that I am well and sound as a brick. I never felt better in my life than at present, and may God grant me the blessing of good health is my sincere wish and prayer.

I have little news to write to you, but it is a pleasant task to write to you, and when I have nuthing to read that interests me time drags slowly away for I do not take much pleasure in visiting out of the company.

We have warmer weather the last two or three days than for the week previous. I will have to tent by myself tonight as the boys are all on duty. It looks as though we might have some rain before morning.

I think I shall be able to build a fort if necessary when I get home, for I have had a chance to visit at evry nook and corner of the one at Hilton Head. I suppose you think as I did when at home. How do men get used to cast off the fear of war and battle? I think I can tell you something about it. By being surrounded by the implements of war and their use and using. Do you suppose the roar of the cannon startles me? Not at all, it is an evry day necessity. We hear something, and sometimes 10, 20, 40 or a hundred a day, and the report of musketry is as common as the chirp of the birds in mid summer.

If you could see the arms and accouterments of war that I have seen since I saw you, you would not wonder that men lose their lives in battle. I suppose there is a dread lump in the heart of nearly evry soldier when led to the field of battle, but that dread wears off by being acustomed to scenes of courage.

You may ask, do I feel the dread of war. As when at home, I would answer, No, but I hope I may never see the field of strife. Yet if God wills it so, I submit. May it please Him to return me to house and friends is my fervent wish, as home and friends are as near and dear to me as dear life itself.

Yesterday was the anniversary of the taking of this place. In the morning there was a salute fired, and I presume there could have been a thousand flags counted, waving the Stars and Stripes with evry breeze. The signal station was decorated with at least 20 flags of different size, and the fleet and boats were draped in their glory. 3 years ago yesterday that island was captured.

Election has come and gone, and may God grant that the best man for the present times has been elected to the Presidential chair is all I have to say or wish about the result. Political party feeling and sore heads will be the result tonight in many cases, but I waive them all as of no account to me or any other good citizen. The Union Constitution and laws of justice and humanity outweigh them all with me.

I would close for tonight if I could find a task more pleasant, but it has been my sincerest pleasure to pen lines to my friends when duty did not fill my time and attention. I have put in more than two months of my twelve, and how checked it looks to cast the thoughts over the road forever gone. As to time, time marches on never to be recalled, but how pleasant the trace it leaves at times, and how rough and thorny at others. Still my hopes sound high at the thought of finding still more pleasant turns in the road that is supposed to lay before us. May it please Him who rules the earth and sky to permit us to tread in the arbour of pleasure and contentment when wars and the rumors of war have died out in the distance as it were, and our distracted and bleeding country may again thrive under the blessings of a permanent peace, and the sword thrown aside, the plow and implements of husbandry take their place. But enough of this, it will soon be roll call time, then evrything else must be thrown aside for a pleasant sleep in the old fashioned bed of slabs.

Our boys at the hospital are nearly all on the gain, and I hope to see them all back to the company soon. There has no mail come here since I wrote to you. We look for the boat tomorrow or next day. Then I hope to hear from home, as hope is the leading string of youth. We must hope on and hope ever.

I presume you will think this a solemncoly letter. Perhaps it is, but you know me too well to be deceived with my gass, so I write as I feel, and I feel first rate at the present time.

I have written several letters for Charley Elmore, and the boys put me up to write in one that he felt as if he could [be] virtuous for the coming year, and he hoped she would be the same. He received her answer last week, and it was true blue. I tell you she allowed that no Terry could fool her as they had Eell's wife. He need have no fears on her account, and she had in there "Dear Charley" 40 times I guess. It was rather rough of me, I will admit, but soldiers will have their fun, cost what it may.

I have heard the character of evry woman, girl, and boy portrayed in pictures of full portrait that ever lived in Colchester, I think, since I came here. The army is rough as the fair [fare] they live on, but as to morality, I was surprised. I think you could not find the same number of men at home and congregate them with no restraint atached that would swear less than they do here, but there is some rough and rough enough.

You must excuse poor writing and mistakes, and I remain as ever your sincere husband.

D.B. White

How I wish I knew you were all well to night. My rest would be sweet then.

On November 8, 1864 Abraham Lincoln was elected to his second term as President. He received over 75% of the military vote and 55% of the total popular vote. General McClellan, "Little Mc" as Daniel called him, was bitter over the defeat, and resigned from military service. Lincoln promoted Philip Sheridan to Major General, Regular Army, to fill the vacancy.

DEAR WIFE

Mrs. Daniel B. White
Downsville, Delaware County, NY

Hilton Head, SC
Saturday, Nov. 12, 1864

Dear Wife,

I take the present opurtunity to write a few lines to you. I am well and tough as tripe in more senses of the word than what is taken in consideration as regards health. I am enjoying the best of health, and what could I enjoy if health was lacking. I sincerely hope that this may find you all enjoying the same blessing.

The mail came to our company today. I received one from Charley & you dated Oct. 21st, & one from you dated Oct. 30th. I have received no letters from any of you between Oct. 2nd & Oct. 21st. Whether you have written none between those dates, I do not know. I want you to be particular about directing. Make the "K" plain. I think some are so near an "H" that they mistake them.

I received a letter from Net White. She says she would be pleased to have you make them a visit. I am glad that John is getting round again, and sorry to hear that your father is unwell. I am afraid that you expose yourself too much. I hope that you will be careful of your health.

I guess you need not mind about hiring out right away, as I think you would be better at home this winter, & then if we see spring then we will speak about it. Visit and enjoy yourself, that is the style for me. But at the same time you must do as you see fit.

You must tell Charley that I cannot write to him this time, but will remember him and shall not write any more to Net until I receive one from .her. I have meant to have written home to see how & where William [White: brother] was, and I am glad you thought to tell me about him. I hope you will see Mother & Jameses folks often, for I think you may be sure you will be a welcome visitor there.

There is none of the boys that went to the hospital back to the company yet, but I think they are all on the gain. Dick Spencer was taken to the hospital today. Corneal Bennett has been off the hooks for a few days, but is round again. There has been three deaths in the 144th this week: [Daniel F.] Eaton of Co. C, Jeremiah Barnhardt of Co. G, & [Milton A.] Young of Co. I.

You thought that I would like to have some sugar & tea sent. Sugar is about as cheap here as there, and we have tea once a day, & we all eat more trash than is good for health. I believe if some that are in the hospital had been out of money, they would be healthy at present. We are apt to eat too much if we eat what tastes good to us. No more. Good by.

Yours ever,
D.B. White

Mrs. Daniel B. White
Downsville, Delaware County, NY

Hilton Head, SC
Saturday, Nov. 12, 1864

Dear Companion,

I will write a few more lines tonight.

The reason that the mail was longer coming last time was on acount of a freshit. The water was so high out at sea that they had to go to shore and tie up for two days. Ask John if he thinks he could snub for the old Fulton. Well, I heard that given as a reason, whether it is so or not I will have you to judge. I know that there is about 10,000 rebel prisoners in transports lying out in the harbor at Hilton Head, & there was 6 carried out and buried here yesterday. The bugle is about blowing roll call, so I will soon have to dig for tall timber.

IT IS A COLD WINTER IN SOUTH CAROLINA

I do not know how we will ever get up in the morning when we get home for we have 3 fifes & 5 drums to make musick for us to get up by now days, and as many to make us go to sleep. Then there is Officer's calls & Fatigue calls, Sergeants calls, drill calls, dress parade calls, breakfast calls, dinner & supper calls, call to get up, & calls to go to bed. There is a time for everything but prepare to die here. Yet we have church calls Sundays.

There is a dance almost every night here. This makes the third night in succession that they have had a dance in our cook house, & hope they will play out soon, that is, so many of them.

I will close for the present. A good night to you, & pleasant dreams.

Sunday, Nov. 13, 1864

I will finish this would be letter. I will have to mail this as I think the mail will close today. We have had company inspection this morning.

I shall send a picture for Ann [Anna Merritt: Amanda's sister] in your letter, & some papers and books for you. I think I shall have to have a dozen fotographs taken. It will cost me $5.00. I think the money would do you more good.

DEAR WIFE

I expect we will get our pay about the middle of the month, but it may be two months before I get it, but I hope not. I have lent so much money that I will have to hold on for a little while.

I have no news to write, so I shall close for the present. We have no victuals to spare. It takes all we draw to keep us in running order. We draw one loaf of bread each day, and a hearty, well man can eat it easy enough at two meals. I have to buy crackers or bread for the third meal often, but I rather buy than to be sick so I cannot eat my rations.

The weather is cool. I suffered last night with cold. I have signed for another blanket, but have not drawn it yet. If I had it, I think I could sleep warm.

Charley said they had dug my potatoes, & they did not turn out verry good.

I have heard that they have drafted in Colchester again, but I have heard no names. I also heard that they were trying to raise a bounty of $800.00 dolls. for each drafted man. Woe unto the man that aids in raising that bounty if it be so.

From your verry best friend
D.B. White

IT IS A COLD WINTER IN SOUTH CAROLINA

Mr. Charles Merritt
Downsville, Delaware County, NY

        Hilton Head, SC
       Wednesday, Nov. 16, 1864

Friend Charles,

  I catch a few moments to write to you once more. I am well and feeling like a buck at present, & so long as I feel as well as I have for the past four weeks, & eat an extra ration evry other day, I am all sound.

  I received your letter last mail, & was glad to hear from you. I will atempt to answer those letters that I have an answer for, & those that do not answer my letters, I say to them, just do the other thing. I am where I ask no odds of any man & verry few women for the next 10 months.

  I am in a tough place, and I am tough in all respects. If I can have the blessing of health, that is the most I care. For all the orders Col. Lewis or any other superior atempts to enforce, I am round for evry time, yet some of the orders look a good deal like tyrany.

  We have to wear our overcoats out to roll call morning and night, let the weather be what it may. When the sun shines it is generally verry warm, yet the night is cool, if it is hot enough days to singe a niger.

I have more clothes and better than I ever had at one time in my life before, but Dan will have to foot the bill in the end. That is what is the matter.

I can tell you that you have no idea of war or the consequence arising from the affect of war, and I sincerely hope you never will. I cannot claim that I have an idea of the suffering that the battle field unfolds to the beholder, yet I have seen something of the life a soldier must lead. There is evrything to degrade the human mind, still there is many Christian privelages. We can atend meeting two or three times each week, and have an abundance of good reading distributed to us each week and 3 or 4 dances to atend if so inclined each week.

The boys that are to the hospital are all getting along well I believe. None have come back to the regiment yet, and there is more going evry few days. We have some sick and some bumming. In our company there is lots that are bumming to get rid of duty. Such I have no pitty for. Corneal Bennett has done no duty for several days past. He had a chill of the ague, but he is better today.

There is no news to write at present. All is quiet here. There is 10,000 reb prisoners on transports lying in the harbour here. They have been there about a week. They take one or two wagon load out and burry them evry day.

> Thursday Evening
> Nov. 17, 1864

All well. You must write, all write, and send word to others to write. The mail boat came in tonight; some will get mail tomorrow.

Yours respectfully,
D.B. White

Mrs. Daniel B. White
Downsville, Delaware County, NY

> Hilton Head, SC
> Friday, November 18, 1864

Dear Companion,

I take the privilege of writing a few lines to you to inform you of the fact that I am well, and I sincerely hope this may find you the same. God knows that I apreciate that blessing, and it is the greatest of blessings to me at the present time, if ever in my past life.

I have swung a sythe nearly evry day for more than four weeks past. I have had to atend to Sunday Inspection and general inspection on other days 3 or 4 times. I shall have work for the next 3 months if I am not changed, and I hope I will not be.

There is rumored that we will have to leave here soon. I hope that rumor will prove false. The boys say that Colonel Lewis never was contented if he did not have his men on a tramp somewhere. We expect to have a Col. for the regiment, but who or when we do not know.

I have got along without going to the guard house yet, but it is a wonder as orders are so strict and so thick here. I have got along with all the officers first rate so far with the exception of the Orderly. I have had a few words with him two or three times, and it was a wonder that I did not have an escort to wait on me to the gard house for what I said to him. If it had proved so, I should have apealed to the Captain, for I do not think I shall be deprived of my rights if I can help it.

I had to give Brigadeer General Pine Bogart a fairish damning this morning. He is chief cook, and he thinks it a bigger position than General Grant occupies. We have had some pretty rough times with cooks since we came, and they have been changed 3 or 4 times. Pine, John Warren, and Milton Stephens are cooks now. Pine told in a tent in the

Company that Corneal Bennett and me was as much trouble as all the rest of the Company, and this morning I made him eat his own words. He has been the kindest to me to day of any man since I came to the company. They can't fool me much if I do not catch them at it. As long as I am round as often as I am at the present time, my rations are small enough, if I have them all. I need an extra loaf of bread evry two days. One loaf lasts me two meals, and it has to do three if I do not buy the third, but I do not complain about buying as long as I have the appetite to eat it.

We expected to get our pay the 15th, but it may not come in a month. If I get my pay, I shall have to send a little home to make up for what I have spent already. I want to come out all strait at the end of the year if possible. If my wages clothes me and keeps me, it will be all I expect.

The mail came today. I received a letter from Jim and one from John Conklin and Jane in company, but none from you. I must conclude that my letters do not go strait or yours come strait. I have written a great many and received verry few in proportion to what I have written. You can tell George, if he has received none from me, that I have written to him long enough ago to have had an answer.

I shall have to close for tonight, as it is near roll call time. We have to be punctual to time. Three minutes too late, and we lose our meal, whether breakfast, dinner, or supper.

I suppose Old Abe is to be our President for the next four years. I cannot say that I am glad, neither did I vote for him. I trust in Providence for the best. The worst has shurley come already.

From your best earthly friend,
D.B. White

Saturday, November 19, 1864

I will write a few more lines to you to day. I think the mail will close to day, perhaps not before tomorrow. There is no news today in camp to note. I was out about an hour to work today. I do not think I shall have to do anything this afternoon. We have had Saturday afternoon to clean up always before.

There was a detail out of the regiment of 64 men to go somewhere after Reb prisoners. They went this morning. They say that they are going to put them in the fort for us to guard. If so, it will take a lot of new guards to take care of them.

The weather has been warm for a few days past. We fixed our tent some yesterday, so I think we will be comfortable if it does not get pretty cold. The fleas have played in for the past few nights. They are the worst customers I ever saw. They will make a fellow get right up and get. When they get on a spree I generally take off my clothes and shake them before going to bed.

IT IS A COLD WINTER IN SOUTH CAROLINA

I have written a letter to James White telling him who I want to colect money from this fall. I should like to get enough colected to have what you want to use, and perhaps I shall want some if the regiment has to wait a month or two for our pay.

Our Captain told us today at dinner that there was some Reb prisoners coming here to be put in the fort today. I shall have to work in there some, and I shall have a chance to see Southriners soon.

I want you to write to me. It does me more good to hear from home than anything I hear. I should like to see you about this time of day I'll bet, and you can bet too on that, for Presidential election is past now, and we will not lose our vote. My lays in my tent yet. I think I shall keep it for next year. There was a lot put in the guard house yesterday from Co. C for fiting about politics, and there is a man walking the color line today for swearing, with a board on his back and breast labeled "swearing".

By and in haste,
D.B. White

P.S. I want to answer J. Conklin's letter before the mail closes, and if I have time, but I will.

DEAR WIFE

Mrs. Daniel B. White
Downsville, Delaware County, NY

Hilton Head, SC
Sunday, Nov. 20, 1864

Dear Wife,

I have written one letter to you & one to Charley this mail, but as the mail does not close until tomorrow, 4 o'clock PM, I thought I would write a few more lines to you. I am well, & hope from the bottom of my heart that this will find you all the same.

I spoke to you about some reb prisoners coming here. They have come. I believe there is 180 of them, all officers, Captains & Lieutenants, some Lt. Colonels. I spoke to you about them going in the Fort. That is not the case. They are stationed about 20 rods from our camp. There has been a lot of our boys detailed this afternoon to put up tents for them. The tents are set on the ground. It is a hard place to sleep with the ground wet under them and nuthing to sleep on. Some have blankets & some have none. They are clothed in all shapes, generally looking pretty rough. It seems hard for them, but they are better provided for than our prisoners would be if in their hands, and at the same time we may see times that we would be glad to have their quarters and be in the 144th at the same time. Col. Lewis told them that if they behaved themselves, he would try to make them as comfortable as possible.

There is over 70 of our men on guard. Our town guard will be relieved by another regiment tomorrow, so it will make our guard duty about the same as before.

It rained nearly all night last night and most of the day today. Buell was out on guard last night & is out tonight. That is tough and in a rain storm too, but there is 4 or 5 detailed out of each company in the same shape.

Our Orderly came to our tent after Buell this afternoon, and I thought he might better have taken me as I have had my sleep every night except one since I came here, but I did not volunteer my service, & he did not ask me to do it. The Orderly has nuthing to do with my time until I am taken off fatigue.

I have had it full as easy as any man in the Company, but I think they will have to call in all the men that detailed out of the regiment to do the guard duty. If so, let it be. I will try to do as the rest do.

I think there will be some johnnies that will feel the efects of cold lead if they stay here long. There is lines drawn, and the Rebs have their ground. After they step over that line, our boys are ordered to shoot them. It looks to me as if I could get away from there, but the next thing will be to get off the island. J. Scott is apointed to call the roll for them four times a day.

I have no news to write to you tonight, so I will close for the present, & if I have anything new in the morning, I will write it to you.

From your friend, well wishes, and would be protector.

Oh for this cruel war to end. The johnnies say that we will have them to fight for four years more if it is the case that Lincoln is elected President, for nuthing but their unconditional fredom will stop the war.

Monday Morning

Rained nearly all night. Looks as though it would all day. How I pitty our guards. It is warm. I do not know what I am going to do today, am not detailed for guard today, yet there is not men to relieve the guard today.

I will send a book this mail, & you can keep it or make a present of it to James or Nett or who you choose.

Yours as ever,
D.B. White

IT IS A COLD WINTER IN SOUTH CAROLINA

Mrs. Daniel B. White
Downsville, Delaware County, NY

Hilton Head, SC
Wednesday, Nov. 23, 1864

Dear Wife,

I will atempt to write a few lines to you this morning. I am well and hope this will find you all the same.

It is rather rough writing here this morning. The ink is froze so I can hardly get enough thawed to write with. We have had two cold nights. After it stopped raining it turned cold. Last night it froze so hard that an eight quart pan full of water was froze in a solid cake, and all the wash dishes in camp that had water in them was froze solid. If there had of been snow on the ground it would have come up to old Delaware County nights.

You will have to try hard to read this, for it is so cold that I have to get up and slap my hands to keep warm, and it is about eleven o'clock in the forenoon, & the sun shines out clear, but the wind is so cold that the sun does not have an impression.

I received a letter from you yesterday dated Oct. the 2nd. If you do not know that, this is November. October was last month & only had 31 days.

DEAR WIFE

I do not write at present to write any news, but to let you know how I get along. I was on guard last night, & perhaps will be tonight. Some have been for the past 3 nights. Those prisoners are raiseing cain with guard duty. It takes between 80 & 90 men to guard them. All the guards have to have their guns loaded now. They did not before. And, if someone does not get shot before two weeks rolls around, I shall be glad. The prisoners behave well so far. I hope they will continue to do so.

I received a letter from R. Christie. You all have heard about the wedding. I will wait till some more pleasant time for my remarks.

I was sorry to hear that you did not get your likeness taken after your trouble. If you could get ½ dozen fotographs, you could send one to me safer than in a case. I cannot see how it takes so long for a letter to come from home here.

If you can sell them sheep, do so, if you do not get more than four shillings for the old sakes. If you want to keep old Dixie, do so, & save hay to winter her.

I am glad you are better, and all the folks tell me what George is doing this winter. Ask him if he wants me to write to him again before he answers mine, also Nett and John.

Amanda, you say you wish you was here to stay with me. Well, I wish you was not. If you could see what I can, you never would wish to play Picket in your life. We have one woman in camp, Capt. [William] Plaskett's wife, and I cannot see the comfort she can take. Rather hope that God will spare our lives to meet in old Delaware, and then I can clasp you to my heart and call you my best friend. May God grant such a meeting.

I have heard this morning that Charles Telford died in the hospital yesterday morning. I think it is true.

I cannot stand to write any more today. I shall try to write you again before the mail closes, but I cannot tell when I can get time since they have put me on guard.

You must write. I am always glad to hear from you & home. Give my respect to all. I hope it will get warmer soon. We feel the cold. It is so warm, then so cold. The boys say that it was full as cold last night as any last winter.

D.B. White

DEAR WIFE

Mrs. Daniel B. White
Downsville, Delaware County, NY

Hilton Head, SC
Thursday, Nov. 24, 1864

Dear Companion,

I have just eaten dinner and feel noble. We have had a Thanksgiving dinner today, potatoes, fresh beef, bread, and coffee. Perhaps you may not think that worth being thankful for, but I do feel thankful for that. It was the best dinner I have eaten in a month and a half. We had to go to church first this morning then atend a review, the 144th and the 25th Ohio. That regiment is on the island with us, and does the town duty now.

It has been cold since I wrote you a couple of days ago, but today is more comfortable. Yet it will be cold tonight. I hope we will not see such cold changes often. The inhabitants of the island say that there has not been a night in three years past that froze ice as thick as last Monday night. The ice in pails, tubs, and other larger vessels was 11½ inches thick.

I came off guard duty yesterday and expect to go on at three o'clock today. If I do, I shall not get this mailed to go this time as the mail will close tomorrow at 4 o'clock PM, and

IT IS A COLD WINTER IN SOUTH CAROLINA

I have just been informed that I shall have to guard prisoners tonight, and if any of them walk over the dead line in front of me, there will be one less to fight some other day.

When we guard prisoners we have to walk our beat two hours, then we have to keep up for two hours more for fear of the Rebs making a dash to escape. It is the worst guard we have. We are on duty 4 hours and off two. Any other, we are on two and off four.

J.D. Scott calls the roll for 49 of them four times each day. He is in my tent writing to send to you at present.

I am well as usual, and if it does not get colder than today, I will be happy.

There is no news, so I will not write any more today. The letters that are sent here takes a month often to come here. I do not know how it is with them going home.

I sincerely hope this will find you all well. Buell says he is going to send a letter home this mail. If you get this before Jane gets one, tell her he is well but awful busy. We send one and often two each mail. I have never missed sending one or two, and sometimes three each mail.

Yours Ever,
D.B. White

DEAR WIFE

> Camp of the 144th Regt.
> Hilton Head, SC
> Nov. 24, 1864

Well Amanda,

Daniel says that you have not seen my parler ornament lately. I hope she is well. I have not heard from hir in some time, but just wait till I git home, and then.

Well Amanda, I am living with the Rebs now. Thair is 198 of them hear, and they make me liv with them all the time. I hav charg of one batalion of them. They are all ofisers, from Colonel down to 2 Lt.. I hav to call the roal four times a day, and the rest of the time I hav to my self.

When you write to Dan, just write a few lines to me and let me know how all the folks is gitting along.

No more at present.

Good Day,
Jim Scott

IT IS A COLD WINTER IN SOUTH CAROLINA

Mrs. Daniel B. White
Downsville, Delaware County, NY

Hilton Head, SC
Tuesday Nov. 29, 1864

Dear Wife,

I seat myself to write a few more lines to you. I am still enjoying the blessing of health. I have caught some cold, & my throat is some sore, but not bad.

We are in a bad sittuation as far as duty is concerned. All the 144th have left except Company D, Company K and a few of Company E, and they are in the Fort. There is some of the Ohio soldiers here, about 75 I think.

We had bad luck last night. There was 4 of the Reb prisoners escaped from us, & they have not been captured yet. It is now about 3 o'clock in the afternoon. I was on guard last night and shall be tonight again.

Things have come to a point when it will accuire all the vigilence that we are master of, & we have not any more than half men enough on the island to do the duty, no, not one man where we should have five.

We were called out to drill at two o'clock, and the Provo Martial came where we were drilling and told us to do no unnesesary duty for we had 240 Rebs to guard and it was nessesary for us to be as vigilent as possible, just as much so as though we were right in front of the enemy, & we had the Rebs to guard, & there was all the force inside the yard that he could depend on, & there is only about 150 of us here. He said it all depended on us whether the Reb prisoners made a rush and escaped. He told us it would be tough, but we must do our whole duty. He said that we must kill evry one that made a suspicious motion, & give no quarter unless they surrendered. He says that he can see that they are bound to escape if possible, & they understand our situation and will do their best.

The fortifications & fort that I have spoke about to you and that we guarded when in camp is without any guards. I was up to camp today, & things look desolate there. There is a few that were sick in each company that stay there.

I hope we will not have the duty long in the shape it is. A small force here could take the island at present. I shall do my duty as long as I can, & then there will be no blame atached to me. I did not let any get out of the prison I guarded last night, neither did any of my reliefs. I took, I presume, 50 to the privy, two at a time, last night.

Those that escaped cut a hole in the floor of their cell and went down through. I have heard since I commensed writing that they have captured them again, but I do not know for certain yet. They report that some darkies picked them up.

I have heard since I commensed writing that James Hotchkiss died this afternoon at the hospital. As to the truth of it I cannot vouch.

I hope this will find you all well and hope to enjoy the same. No more at present, for I expect to be too late for to catch the mail.

From your ever true friend & husband,
Daniel B. White

P.S. I shall write as soon as possible again.

On November 16, 1864 General Sherman left Atlanta and began his march to the sea. He cut all communication with Union headquarters, and, with 62,000 men divided into two wings, started sweeping across Georgia toward Savannah. There was little Confederate opposition along the way. The forces under General John Bell Hood harassed the rear of his columns for a time, but less than 10,000 soldiers stood in his path.

Sherman believed the battle for Savannah would be a hard one. Confederate General William J. Hardee, who commanded Savannah and central Georgia, was a respected opponent. Hardee was already reinforcing the defenses around Savannah in preparation for battle.

Sherman requested that Major General Foster break the Charleston and Savannah railroad. If the rail link could be destroyed, Savannah would be nearly isolated. Union forces had held Fort Pulaski at the mouth of the Savannah River since April of 1862. If Fort McAllister, controlling another approach to the city, could be taken, escape or resupply by sea would be difficult. With the railroad gone the danger of resupply from (or escape toward) Charleston would be minimized. General Hardee and his troops could be captured at Savannah.

Daniel White, in his letter of November 29, 1864, tells us that most of the 144th have left. General Foster and 5,500 of the men under his command set off from Hilton Head, up the Broad River on transports. He planned to destroy the rail line somewhere near Grahamsville, South Carolina. At the time, Foster was suffering from an old war wound, and didn't feel he was physically capable of leading a field exercise. He put his troops under the command of Brigadier General John P. Hatch. Foster was with them on the transports, but Hatch was given command of the field operation.

Historians vary in their assessment of the causes, but the mission was not successful from the Union viewpoint. Foster, in his official report, blamed the river pilots for getting them lost in the fog. Others blame the incompetence of Foster or the overly cautious behavior of General Hatch. Still others fault the inexperience of the Union soldiers. Whatever the reasons, the Federal troops were defeated and the mission failed. The rail line was defended by just a few soldiers when

IT IS A COLD WINTER IN SOUTH CAROLINA

Foster left Hilton Head, and could have been broken by a quick decisive movement, but delays allowed the Confederate forces to learn of the Union's approach and to send for reinforcements, which General Hardee sent from Savannah. In fact, some of the forces which Hardee sent had just come from Charleston on the very same rail line.

Engagements at Boyd's Neck, Honey Hill, Deveaux Neck, and Tullifinney River took place between November 30th and December 9th. At the end of that period Hatch's men had managed to gain a position where they could destroy anything moving on the railroad, but they never succeeded in breaking the line.

General Sherman's troops captured Fort McAllister and besieged Savannah. On December 21st, the morning they were to make their final assault, they found the city deserted. General Hardee and his outnumbered army had escaped toward the north.

Daniel White's letters of early December tell us what he knows of Sherman's progress and the battles as he learns the details in camp. They illustrate just how little the common soldier, even one at a headquarters unit, knew about what was happening around him.

It is also interesting to note that while Daniel reports the war news as he hears it, he quickly returns to more familiar ground, his duties, the mail, and thoughts of home.

There is a minor mystery here as well. In his letter of November 29th, Daniel reported the death of James Hotchkiss, a Private in Company K. Indeed, the National Cemetery at Beaufort, South Carolina agrees. Their records indicate that James Hotchkiss was interred on November 30, 1864, and there is a headstone in the cemetery inscribed with his name *and regiment. However, the "Descriptive Book of the 144th Regiment" lists Private James Hotchkiss as having been discharged with the regiment in July, 1865. In addition, "Back in War Times", the regimental history, shows him living in Downsville, New York when that book was written in 1903.*

Mrs. Daniel B. White
Downsville, Delaware County, NY

Hilton Head, SC
Thursday, Dec. 1, 1864

Dear Wife,

I seat myself to write a few more lines to you. I am well at present, and sincerely hope this may find you all enjoying the same blessing.

Dear friend it will be sad news to you, and many sad hearts will beat in unison in Del. Co. when you and many others hear from the 144th next time. There is many sad hearts here today. If the report is true, the 144th boys, many of them, have bit the dust. I cannot give you any particulars that are reliable, but this much I do know, that there are many wounded that have passed near our barricks today. I have seen a train of ambulances passing to and from the hospital carrying wounded soldiers to the hospital for the past three hours at least, and some that were wounded too badly to ride are carried on streachers.

Oh, the bitter anguish this cruel war is causeing in our land. Our regiment left camp Monday night, and could not have been absent from the dock more than 24 hours before they were engaged in what is supposed here at present a terrible battle for the number engaged, and it is supposed the Rebs had double our force. I do not remember the name of the place at present, but will give you some more particulars before closing.

There has up to the present time about 150 wounded been sent back here, but you must understand that all those are not from our regiment Yet I think I can say with truth that our regiment and the 25th Ohio has suffred severely. The loss of ours last night, as given by our officers that have returned wounded at 4 PM, was supposed to be about 250, and they are supposed to be still fighting and, when last heard from, not having gained their object.

There has been sealed orders sent here by General [John G.] Foster to have a large supply of amunition sent and some seige guns, with twenty days more rations for the men, and they took 25 days rations with them. The suplies sent for were sent this morning. It may be possible that we will have to follow them. If so, I will try to mail this and inform you if

I go. For that reason, I write now. I think we will not be likely to go unless there is others sent to take our place here, for we have more than we can do a long period of time where we are.

There is about one half of our company and Co. D. that have slept only 2 nights in seven. I have been more lucky than many of the boys, for I did not do duty at camp when some others did. I have been on duty every other day since last Friday. I was on duty last night, and do not feel verry slick today. I have a cold in my head, and feel as though I had been on a regular spree. We cannot sleep verry much when on guard, for we have to stand 2 hours then have 4 to lay down, and by the time we get to sleep, another relief has to be called, then that wakes us all up again. But we do not complain, for it looks at present as though we had been greatly favoured to get the position we now occupy, and I trust God will protect me still, and hope for the best as it concerns myself and companions.

I would give you a list of names of the killed and wounded as we have heard them, but I will wait, trusting that I can be more fully informed before the mail leaves here. There is some wounded that I have seen. It is reported that nearly all of Co. G is among the captured, but I hope not, Jonas and Enos More is in that company.

IT IS A COLD WINTER IN SOUTH CAROLINA

Friday, Dec. 2, 1864

Rumors of all kinds concerning our regiment; not as bad as suposed at first.

Saturday, Dec. 3, 1864

Better news from the boys: 68 killed and wounded; 14 killed.

Sunday, Dec. 4, 1864

Report from the front -- All has been quiet since the first atack. Some of our officers came here today from the front report 81 killed, wounded, and missing; 68 killed and wounded; 14 killed; severe loss among the noncommisioned oficers; nearly half of the killed are officers. I have heard some names of the killed and wounded, but will probably get the official report before the mail closes.

The Arago came in tonight. Hiram Gray [is] with us. He brought me good news and something better, your picture. I just felt noble, and was as tickled to see my old spouse as a boy with a new jackknife, and it was better than I supposed. There was my old friend Carrie, natural as life. I want you to send me directions so I can send her or her father a letter and thank her for her kindness, and I wish to send a letter to her father as he requested me to do so. When I get back,

I'll bet we will make them a visit, won't we. I will close for the present. Good by.

Monday, Dec. 5, 1864

We are all feeling good, better than you could supose under the circumstances. We have been on guard four days in succession, and not relieved in that time, but for the past day we have had four reliefs, so we are off the beat six hours and on two. We do not complain, and can stand it in that shape for a week to come, but it will wear us out after a while.

The Ohio boys have gone to the front, so it leaves us to do the duty here. There is a few recruits here that are waiting for transportation to their regiments. They have armed them to make the fourth relief.

I will send another letter with this, and the same mail, so you will need both to find the news.

Yours as ever,
D.B. White

I have written before about our situation and garding Reb prisoners and about four of them escaping from us. Instead of it being four it was six. There has been four of them captured by darkies and brought back, and the other two treed. So, this forenoon there was six men detailed to go after them. Buell Robinson went, and they have just come back not more than three minutes ago with the other two. So, we have them all once more.

What men is here on duty is nearly all that are on the island, except the citizens. The citizens have been enrolled to do duty and was armed here last Monday, and do guard duty in town and dock and on the breastworks, but the place is poorly guarded at present. The magazines near our old camp are not guarded at all. It would give any person feeling malicious a chance to do us a great deal of injury. I hope it will not prove so, trusting that the ruler of an all wise Providence will do all things well.

I leave you for the present, and will endeavour to give you particulars of all the affairs that has befallen us. Sad it is, but we must submit. Had any person told me a week ago that we would be where we now are, that our regiment would be called to bleed on the field of strife, I should thought they were fools or worse than fools, but so it is. We know not when we are in danger. I cannot say that we are more safe here than the other boys are where they are.

Oh, for this war to cease and peace and unity to reign once more.

We have been all excitement for fear of the prisoners trying to make a dash on us and escape. We have been under arms ever since the regiment left, but all is quiet yet.

DEAR WIFE

Mrs. Daniel B. White
Downsville, Delaware County, NY

Hilton Head, SC
Monday, Dec. 5, 1864

Dear Wife,

I still have time to write, and it is a pleasure for me to do so. I have just finished a letter of two sheets, all that will go in one envelope, and I want to write some more, so I think I can fill two more before the mail closes which will be 4 or 5 days. You must give the rest some of your news as I cannot write to any of them at present. Tell them I would be happy to do so if I could.

Dec. 6, 1864

Tuesday morning finds me well, that is, healthy, but about worn out. I have not been relieved from guard duty for the past five days, and do not expect to be relieved for five more to come.

I was called out of my quarters yesterday, and my writing was cut short in a hurry. The Provo Martial called us all out and talked to us, and told us that it stood us all in hand to be prepared for a fight any minute, and keep our arms so we could reach them any moment. The prisoners have been caught twice before, and yesterday, in a conspiracy, calculating to overpower the guards and take the island or escape from us. The Provo Martial had good reason for suspecting that they were going to have help from the outside, and he prepared for a dash on the guards. He sent for all the men he could command here at present. There was about 150 men under arms last night, all night, but we are all right yet. Whether it requires all the vigilance we have here or not, I do not know, but I presume that those officers that we have prisoners would like nobly to leave, and we are bound to relieve them from this world if they try to escape.

The news received yesterday from the boys up in the front was good. They had captured one Battery and gained some ground, and it is reported that Sherman was at Savannah and gave them yesterday to remove the women and children. This morning he commences to beseige Savannah, if there is no other arrangements since yesterday, and our boys were going to try to capture a railroad bridge that the cars run over leading from Richmond to Charleston. I hope the boys will soon be back, for their sakes and ours too, for it will wear us out shortly to do the duty here. But, enough war news. I suppose you will care little about such news, only so far as it concerns us all.

I received my mail yesterday, and received one from Robert Scott. He sent a paper, so he said, in his letter, but I did not receive it. I have received no letters with a list of the drafted and only one from Nett and eight from you, counting those in envelopes with others. Hiram Gray has not got his box up to our quarters yet. I hope you will not send me many things. I cannot tell how long I will be here. I am sorry to hear that our folks have been troubled so much with sickness since I left home, but hope you may all enjoy good health in the future.

You speak of soldiers hurting themselves, eating and drinking. There is no danger here, for we do not get anything to drink here but coffee or tea, and nothing to eat to speak of but bread and occasionally a little salt hoss or pork, which I scarcely ever taste, and hominy once a week, and peas or beans once or twice a week, but if you was here you could not tell by seeing the boys but they had sweet cake and gingerbread.

The war news is good from all sections, so we all feel good, hoping to reach home and friends soon. Oh, what a happy day that would be, but all of the suffering we expect to endure before that happy time. My earnest wish is God grant that we may stand the trial and win the [peace] back to our country and friends. Do not suppose by my writing in this shape that I am downhearted or I feel downhearted, for I feel most noble and like a fighting cock, and trust that I shall see old Delaware County again.

I think there is no danger of my sending any Williams' letters. I should be afraid that a son sent in that way would be likely to be born with a musket in his hand and a hard tack in his mouth. You can tell Polly Jane so, if you chose.

I shall send another sheet with this, and then I can find time perhaps to tell you some more news and how our regiment is situated, and will try to get a list of the names of the killed, wounded, and missing.

I think that Isac Williams will feel noble when he hears of having such a son, who would not. I must bid you good bye, and have good courage for I am coming round all right.

Ever yours,
D.B. White

Mrs. Daniel B. White
Downsville, Delaware County, NY

Hilton Head, SC
Tuesday, Dec. 6, 1864

Dear Friend,

I take my pen in hand this morning to finish writing the letter I commensed yesterday. I am still round, but feel pretty nearly whipped. I hope to be relieved tomorrow so I can get one night's rest in a week, but I may not be. If not, I shall try it longer.

There is no news of importance this morning. I did not hear anything from the regiment yesterday. I do not know that I can get a list of the names of the boys that have suffered in the fight they have been in, but I will soon. Things are going off all quiet here yet. Sometimes I hope they will, at other times I wish the Rebs would try to break out. I think there would be less to guard before they got through.

I have heard just now that the boys were fighting again. I am sorry to hear that, but hope and trust they will come out top of the heap. I suppose I am doing wrong writing such news home, but you may know the worst as well now as ever. Do not worry about it until you hear all the particulars. We all hope that things will be better in the end, that it looks now that is generally the case. We hear all the worst in times of an excitement. I think there is a better prospect of the war ending now than at any time since it commenced.

Buell Robinson has been unwell for a few days past, but nuthing dangerous I suppose, just worn out and comfortably sick.

I suppose the snow will be blowing round you in Old Delaware, and it is comfortably warm here. Since we came down here there has been no rain, but I think we will have some today. It has been so warm since we came here that I have not suffered any lying out in the open air, but we have a guard house for some of the guards. Some lay on the stoop of the Provo Martial's house. We have a shelter over head, and do not mind lying in the open air. We should not complain when we think how many suffer so much more than we do. I am contented when I think of the boys that are up in the front or in Grant's army with cold weather, perhaps snow for a bed.

I think I shall have to close for the present. I must try to write one more letter more today to Nelly Nichol. I have not answered hers yet. I would like to write one to James White, but think I cannot do so this mail. Keep up good courage, and I will try to take care of myself as well as I can, for you do not want me to come home more than I want to. Yours ever the same,

D.B. White

DEAR WIFE

Mrs. Daniel B. White
Downsville, Delaware County, NY

Hilton Head, SC
Saturday, December 10, 1864

Dear Wife,

I take a few moments tonight to write to you. I am well, and how sincere is my wish that this may find you all the same. I was off the hook a little one day on acount of being tired out, but a day & night rest brought me round all right again.

We are still guarding the Rebs, and have all we had and several more. Our boys are at a place called Honey Hill, and see lots of rebs evry day, and have had three or four skirmishes with them since I last wrote to you. I fear that the 144th will be a small regiment before they get back. We have a list of the sufferers in the first fight, but nuthing later. One of the Co. K boys that went as Color Corporal was killed day before yesterday, Cyrus Hotchkiss.

I received some mail last night, one letter from Wm. White. He is well and in good spirits. I also received a letter from Nett White, none from Hamden or Colchester. The Fulton will be here tomorrow or next day perhaps. Then I hope to hear from home. I commensed writing a letter to James to send last mail, but did not have time to finish it.

We have been here over two weeks, & I have been off duty only one day. I am sitting up to take my post at 10 o'clock. I will come off at 12, then I shall try to sleep some. We are all on guard in just that shape off about one day in 9 or ten.

I do not know when the mail will leave here. My last mail came on a small boat running from New York to this place. If she sails before the Fulton, she will take the mail. I may write more, and I will try to get a paper to send with an acount of the fight, but that, perhaps, I cannot do. I think the More boys are all right so far, and Jonas is in camp.

I will have to close for the present as it is near my time to dig out. The weather has been fine since the cold snap we had in camp until last night. It rained some. It is cool tonight, and the wind blows hard. We had a heavy wind night before last, and yesterday the sand blew as thick as snow has at any time in Delaware County.

I bid you an affectionate good night, trusting that we may see the time that we will not be obliged to converse with pen & paper and thousands of miles between us.

DEAR WIFE

Monday evening
December 12, 1864

I will take my pen in hand for a few minutes again. I am well tonight. There is nuthing new here at present. We had a verry cold tedious night last night, but it is warmer tonight. Citizens say that they never saw as cold weather before at this place.

Some boys from the 157th NY came here from the front with some prisoners. They say that the boys there has had a rough time, & say that they never saw men fight as our boys did up there. They say that they could not be drove. The news from there is good so far, and we hear that Sherman is at Savannah. If that is the case, it will be a noble victory. There was a salute fired today in honor of the event.

We expect the Fulton here tomorrow. I received a letter from James today. It was sent up to the front then back again. I cannot write any more to night. I will leave space for some other news that I may wish to write before closing.

Yours as ever,
D.B. White

Tuesday, December 13, 1864

I will have to close as the mail leaves here this afternoon. The Fulton came last night, but I do not know whether I will get mail or not.

IT IS A COLD WINTER IN SOUTH CAROLINA

There is no news of importance. We have heard nuthing from the front. I will send a letter when the Fulton leaves. That will be 3 or 4 days.

I remain your truest friend,
D.B. White

Mrs. Daniel B. White
Downsville, Delaware County, NY

Hilton Head, SC
Thursday, Dec. 15, 1864

Dear Wife,

I wish to inform you that I am well, & hope that this will find you all enjoying that same blessing.

I have no news of note to write to you at present, but as the mail closes today, I cannot bear to let it go without sending you a letter, for I know that you will be anxious to hear from Hilton Head. There is no news of account from our boys or Sherman. We have heard that our boys are preparing to have a battle, and we expect to hear from them today.

We lose some men evry day, but the boys hold their ground. At last account they command the Savannah and Charleston Railroad, and hold Pocotaligo Bridge, but I cannot say that we have gained anything that we may not lose again.

I have to inform you of the death of Peter Littlejohn; he was shot through the head. John Salton was wounded in the hand. Peter Penny came here day before yesterday. He had been home on a sick furlough. He has staid with me since he came, but when he will have to go to his company, I do not know.

I received some things in a box that came to the Conklin boys: a pair of socks, a pair of mittens, some dried blackberries, and I should think 12 or 15 pounds of butter. I am pleased to think that I have friends at home so kind, and am verry much obliged to all for their kindness. If I stay here any length of time, they will all come good. I have tasted butter only three times before. The butter is good. We hardly have time to stew berries, but I shall have some time.

I received nuthing that came in a box that came to Hiram Gray, but I have not called for anything. I hope you will not take the trouble you have been to to send me things. They all come good, but it has been too much trouble to you.

I received a box of pills, or part of a box, that came with Gray. I was sick a day or two after, and I think those same pills saved me a rough time. I hate so bad to go to the doctors for their medicine, and they seem to kill more than they cure, and we are worse off here than when at camp. I do not like our doctor that is in the Provo Yard. I came around all right in 12 hours after I took a good dost of pills.

I have no time to write more at present. I have been hardly ten minutes writing this, and you will be surprised to think it took me so long.

I have a few minutes to eat a piece, then I have to go on guard. Do not worry about me. If I have to go to the front, I trust God to spare my life there the same as here. Perhaps I will not have to go. Put your trust in Providence knowing that He dooeth all things well.

Your sincere friend and husband,
D.B. White

CHAPTER FOUR

MERRY CHRISTMAS

Mrs. Daniel B. White
Downsville, Delaware County, NY

Hilton Head, SC
Sunday, Dec. 25, 1864

Dear Wife,

I wish you a Merry Christmas. I have just come in off guard and eat my dinner. That was a short job. We had bread, coffee, and a little hash made from the remainds of a dead ox.

I wish I could write some news, but I have no news to write. Things go off just as usual. I have heard that all our regiment was captured, but that is not so I think. I suppose that it is true that they have moved, but where I cannot tell.

MERRY CHRISTMAS

The general opinion is that they are going to operate with Sherman against Charleston. There is little use conjecturing anything until we hear from good authority. We cannot tell when we will be called to join the regiment.

We have some help here now. There is a squad of Darkies here that do guard duty. They may stay one day, and they may stay a week. Sometimes there is not more than 50 men in this yard except our company and Co. D. At other times there is 3 or 4 thousand here. I presume there is 2,000 here today, most of them discharged soldiers waiting for transportation home.

The Rebs are pretty downhearted since the fall of Savannah.

Well my youthful friend, what is the prospect, how do you think you will enjoy the holiday season. Are you thinking anything about going to Westfield this New Years. I think the prospect looks poor for me going there this year. I wish I could and have the same crowd with an additional few that was not there last year. But never mind, when this cruel war is over, and I return home once more, I think we will enjoy the blessings and comforts of home better than ever before for the reason that I will know better how to apreciate the blessings of home and society of friends.

DEAR WIFE

You must tell Nett that I received her letter and will answer it next mail if nuthing happens. Tell her to write to me in English style next time.

I believe George Warren is going home on a furlough. He expects to start Tuesday. Tell Nett that if she does not send her picture before he comes back to send it with him.

I have written letters to go this mail to George and John and R. Scott. Tell Jim and Charles that I will remember them boys; tell Papa John and my old Mamma-in-Law that I send my best respects to them. Tell Sarah to write if Bill does not. Tell Anna that I send my love to her.

The boys all feel pretty good now. I saw Ed White and Charley Bogart. They are getting along fine. I have not heard anything from Billie McDonald for a few days, but suppose he is getting better.

I will have to close as we are ordered to go to the guard house, and stay there and have the promise of being relieved tomorrow. Just eat a little roast turkey and charge it to me.

Our boys brought in a drownded man this morning, but who he was I do not know.

I must bid you a good by. May you enjoy yourself is the sincere wish of your truest earthly friend.

D.B. White

When you get my big letter, let me know. You will have some days reading them.

Mrs. Daniel B. White
Downsville, Delaware County, NY

Hilton Head, SC
Friday, Dec. 30, 1864

Dear Wife,

It is with pleasure that I take my pen in hand to write a few more lines to you. I am well, & sincerely hope this may find you all the same.

I have received no letter from you since I received one dated Dec. 6th. I have received none from you the last two mails. I intended to have one the last mail, but no. Well, I can't help it. If they don't come, I won't be troubled reading them. I think I cannot answer Nett's this time. Tell her I want to wait until I have lots of time and gass.

I can write no news of importance. The regiment is up at the front yet. I think we will have to go to Savannah with General Foster, but there is nuthing certain about it.

The boys here have a story going the rounds for the past week that C, D, & K are to go to Elmira to guard some prisoners that are to be sent from here. You may alow that all such stories are gass. I don't want to go north at present. Neither does scarcely any of the boys. We would all freeze stiff before we got that far north. I would like to go to Elmira if I could stay there the remainder of my time, but to go there and turn around and come back would be a rough job at this time of the year.

I have heard today that our Captain [J. Rich] & the Captain of Co. D [E. Griffith] are trying to have the two companies detached to do guard duty in the Provo Yard. Whether they will succeed or not I cannot tell. If they should, it would be a lucky streek for us, as least so it looks at present.

Our Captain was home on a furlough and came back night before last. He was a tickled boy to find Company K here. He supposed we were at the front.

MERRY CHRISTMAS

I have heard the reason Col. Lewis did not take Co. C, D, & K was that some men in each company had made threats that if Col. Lewis ever took them where they could have a chance, they would relieve him of his life. That may be so, but I cannot credit that story.

I shall close for the present. George Warren intends to go home on a furlough. He will start tomorrow or next day.

I think our duty is not so hard as it was. A lot of Darkies relieves us evry other day. The weather has been cool for a few days.

Saturday, Dec. 31, 1864

I am well today and hope this will find you all the same. I have no news. The mail boat leaves this afternoon or tomorrow morning. I am on guard today.

The Rebs think that they would like to have the war close. That is just what I want to hear. Then I might go home. That would be all right, would it not. Still I trust God will bring things round all right in his own good time.

My love to all. I bid you all a hearty good by, and would like to be with you to spend New Years.

From your ever true friend,
D.B. White

DEAR WIFE

===

Mrs. Daniel B. White
Downsville, Delaware County, NY

Hilton Head, SC
Sunday, Jan. 8, 1865

Dear Wife,

    I seat myself to write a few lines to you once more. I still enjoy the blessing of good health, and I hope this may find you still all the same.

    Our company received some mail today. I received one letter from J. Conklin and one from J. White, but none from home. Oh, how I wish I could get one from you once more. The last was dated December 6th. But I will not give it up for I think you cannot be to blame. I feel asured that you write and the Postmasters lose my mail.

    We are still in the Provo Yard. Our regiment came back to camp yesterday morning. I was up to see the boys today. They all seem to feel good and happy to get back again. They seem to think that fighting johnnies is no better than it is called. They say that they will not complain about style if they are permitted to stay in camp the rest of their time, but I missed some of the boys. Where are they? Just where thousands of others are. They have found a resting place beneath a Southern soil. Peter Littlejohn--I miss him. I can hardly give up that I shall see him no more, forever. He was a good boy. Yet such is war.

The officers in companies D & K are trying to have us go back to the regiment. How it will work I cannot tell. We will know before long.

The boys that were with Col. Lewis speak very highly of him.

I have no war news to write. I have heard it reported that Wilmington had fallen into our hands. I hope that it is so.

I cannot tell how long our regiment will stay here. They may not. General Foster took his family to Savannah to let them see the place and see how they would like to live there. I have heard that they did not like it. Foster [says] he is not going to change his headquarters. He had said that the 144th would go where he did, and he was going to keep them with him the remainder of their time.

Adjutant General [Edward] Potter has made his headquarters at Hilton Head, and he wanted Gen. Foster to promise that if he moved to Savannah then he would leave the 144th with him. Foster told him that he had said that the 144th would go where he did, but he would not insist on their going if Potter insisted on their staying with him at Hilton Head, as he would be there a part of the time himself even if he made Savannah his headquarters.

DEAR WIFE

The 144th and the 25th Ohio did not agree very well while at the front. We relieved them in the Provo Yard, and that did not suit them. They called our boys "Foster's Pets". I hope we are all right.

I have heard tonight that there would be no doubt but Foster would go to Savannah. If he does, I think we will be very likely to go with him. We are situated at present in just such a shape that there is no use of conjecturing when or where we will go. A short time after this will tell.

They are putting on more style than we have seen for some time past. We have to drill the day we are off duty. I had about as liff be on guard every day. We are in a regular stampede at present. All the officers in the Department are trying to better their position. The ones that have the most influence with the General will come out first best.

I shall have to close tonight. Perhaps I can find time to write more before closing. Tell all our folks that I will write to them soon.

Jim writes to me that him and Et are going to make you a visit and take you home with them. Enjoy yourself while you can.

MERRY CHRISTMAS

New Years was a dull time here, and cold. I have suffered with cold full as much here as I would if I had been at home.

Your friend as ever,
D.B. White

Mrs. Daniel B. White
Downsville, Delaware County, NY

Hilton Head, SC
Thursday, Jan. 12, 1865

Dear Wife,

I seat myself to write a few more lines to you to inform you that I am still enjoying good health, & hope that this may find you all enjoying the same inestimable blessing.

I received a letter from you dated December 30th at my old fireside. Would to God I could have been there with you, but circumstances will not admit so I will wish you a pleasant time, & I will do my duty with patience & hope for the best.

DEAR WIFE

Friday, Jan. 13, 1865

I had to quit writing last night for supper, & after supper I had to go on guard. We have lost some help, & I have to be on guard all the time. For what I know, one relief is going to receive Secretary [of War, Edwin M.] Stanton. They are just starting. I came on the relief that has to stay here today.

I shall have to stop for the present as it is nearly time for my relief to fall in. I shall finish as soon as I can find time.

Saturday, Jan. 14, 1865

I will try again this morning to see if I cannot find time to finish this miserable letter. I am well with the exception of a lame back. I still enjoy the privelage of standing guard.

Some of the boys have gone to the dock again this morning to see Secretary Stanton. I wish he would come or say that he is not coming. They have kept the regiment in a flurry for the past three days.

Things move here about as usual. We had an addition to our Reb family last night of about 50 men. Nearly 200 of the Reb privates have taken the oath of aligience since they came here. Many more wish to.

MERRY CHRISTMAS

I cannot find time to write to any person at present. I suppose the boys will think I have forgotten them, but I will remember them when I get time.

This is the poorest representation of letter writing I have done in some time, but I think you will excuse me under the circumstances.

The Fulton came in night before last, but I received no letters. The Fulton reported that the Mellville had sunk coming round Cape Hatteras. If so I presume I lost some mail that would be likely to be aboard. I would wait until the boys come back from the dock if I thought they would bring any news as I have written none in this letter. When you read this, that is if you can, you will be justified in burning it without any ceremony.

I think you will get tired reading such letters as I have written to you for some time past.

I remain as ever your sincere friend and husband,
D.B. White

& don't forget to write.

DEAR WIFE

Mrs. Daniel B. White
Downsville, Delaware County, NY

> Hilton Head, SC
> Sunday, Jan. 15, 1865

Dear Friend,

I will write a few more lines to you this morning. I am well, & can eat my rations just as well as I ever could.

There has been a supposed case of the Small Pox in the Provo Yard. One of our Darkies was removed to the Small Pox hospital. Whether he had it or not I cannot tell. Our company had to be vaxinated by order of the Captain. I hope that we will not have to stand a tour of Small Pox.

The great & renowned Secretary Stanton arived at Hilton Head yesterday, but our boys claim that he is only a man in appearance. Stanton, General Sherman, Secretary Chase, General Potter, General Foster, General [Milton S.] Littlefield, & their staff were in company, and the boys said that Col. Lewis had on more style than any of the croud. I think Col. Lewis might get along with less style than he puts on, but he may suit himself. That will suit me.

I have heard that our company had been detailed to do the duty here with Co. D for help. Our company furnishes

MERRY CHRISTMAS

50 men for duty, & Co. D furnishes 27 men. We are on duty all the time for the past four or five days, & the prospect is that we will be on duty all the time for the next month. We have four reliefs, so we are on two hours & off six. We can stand to do duty some time if we have four reliefs. We have one relief of Darkies.

The weather is cool, but we have had no storms for the past ten days. We have verry good quarters & have a stove so we are comfortable. When we are on duty or on post we have to get up once or twice each night, but I am getting used to that, & do not mind it.

Some one of you wanted me to let you know what had become of Bill Johnston. He is in the hospital. I believe I saw him in the Provo Yard one day about two weeks ago. I have heard nuthing from him since. He was better then. Billie was verry sick when he went to the hospital.

We have plenty of company. In our room there is nine of us: Buell, Lorenzo D. Minor, Philo Allison, Hiram Townsend, Charles Lancaster, Chauncy Minor, Erastus Fuller, & myself. So, you may conclude we have a civil croud. George Johnson is the noisiest man in Company K, I think. Still there is some that is not far behind.

Our Company enjoy good health at present. Ed White is in the hospital yet. I see Thomas White evry few days, & William Holmes. He comes in the yard to see us evry few days. I saw several of the Co. E boys day before yesterday. That company is in a fort just outside the Provo Yard. Lora [Lorenzo] Wood & Peter Boyce are in that company.

I shall have to close for the present as I have failed in writing any news. Write & tell evrybody to write, & I remain your sincere friend.

D.B. White

———

Mrs. Daniel B. White
Downsville, Delaware County, NY

Hilton Head, SC
Sunday, Jan. 22, 1865

Dear Companion,

I am well; how are you? My folks are well here; how are they at home?

I received a letter from you yesterday, & was I not a happy boy to hear from home once more. I had not received any mail for two weeks before. I expect that I lost some mail when the steamer Melville sunk coming round Cape Hatteras.

MERRY CHRISTMAS

That was a sad catastrophe, but there was not many passengers aboard.

The boys in Co. K are all getting along as well as the most sanguine might expect. Fet [Lafayette] Hunter has had a hard time. He has been sick nearly all the time since we came here, & he has been dangerous, but is some better now.

We had some new recruits for our company last night. Asel [Asahel] Brainard & Geo. Hawk came here on the Arago yesterday. The 144th must be a noble regiment or they would not get so many recruits.

A part of the regiment were down to the dock today to salute Quartermaster General Meigs. Col. Lewis, I think, likes that business. He is bully for style. There was none from the Provo Yard on that ocasion.

We have had four or five wet days. The weather is cooler today than it has been for two weeks past. We are on duty evry day & have only three reliefs. We have to stand on post 8 hours out of each 24. Our Darkies have left us, and I am glad of it if they have taken the Small Pox with them. There has been two cases reported among them, but they perhaps had none. Things are easily reported in camp.

I have been standing on guard for the past four or five days in front of the Provo Martial's office, & have to salute officers about half the time & read passes the other half. If you could see me you would think I was Brigadier Brindle I guess, with my Government harness & white cotton gloves on and all the rest of my asumed style.

Well I must tell you what conversation I held with two young ladies this forenoon. They were coons. I'll bet you better believe they had their style. They went into the Provo Martial's for a pass to go aboard the Arago, and when they came back I requested them to show me their pass, and they said they had a pass to go on the Arago but I was not the Arago. I alowed that I had not so much stem & stern as the Arago, but I must see their pass. One of them gave me a pass alowing that two ladies might pass on board the boat, signed by the Provo Martial, so I had to let them go. Such incidents are of rare ocurance, but they all go to show what breaks the monotiny of a soldier's life. I have sport with some of the native Darkies that come for passes. They, or some of them, know a little more than old Ring.

Our Rebs are all going to die if they are kept here. I think they leave pretty fast. They ocasionaly get hold of a cat or dog, and dress them & cook & eat them. They are meat hungry I think.

They have 6 of the officers locked up in a cell for stripping one of their officers that they supposed had taken the oath of Alegience. The cells are made of logs, and the floor is made out of logs about 10 inches through, split in four parts, and all the edges are laid up so it makes a rib bed. The cells are about 4 ft. one way & 8 the other. The logs are laid so that the ocupant has to lay croswise on the sharp edges.

I must go to the gard house. Good by.

Monday, Jan. 23, 1865

I will try to write a few more lines today, but I presume there will be a call for me at the guard house before I get fairly commensed. That is the case generally.

We had another verry wet night last night, & cold chilly air, but I was better off than some of my neighbours as I have a sentry box to stand in when it is rainy, so long as I stand in front of the Provo's.

A sentry has a busy time there today. I guess evrybody wants a pass, & I have to quarrel enough of my time to keep me fighting mad, but my fighting weight is not so heavy as it was when I left home. I think I would weigh about 125 lbs. now. I have lost 15 or 20 lbs. since I came here.

You informed me that you were not going to W. Elwood's. I am not sorry about that. I do not want you to hire out to work in a dairy for next summer unless you think you are going to suffer for bread, at least not where there is as much work to do as there was at Avery's or Neishe's. Let me know what you intend to busy yourself with.

You spoke about lending money. Perhaps I may have been pretty pointed in that letter concerning money matters. You must recalect that you make your home for the present at J. Merritt's, and you must use reason about these matters so neither party will be the loser in the end, and you need favours ocasionaly, so I & you must expect to grant some. I have no fears as to your squandering anything. I have heard enough about that lately. Jane wrote to Buell telling him that you sold those old sheep to Polly for $3.00 per head. Buell asked me one night what I had offered them for. I told him I had said that I would take $1.00 apiece for the old ones. The boys in our tent got ahold of the story, and I have heard about your calculating several times since. They alow that when I get home I must let you wear the breeches.

Order. Report to the guard house imediately.

Monday Evening
Jan. 23, 1865

I must close my letter writing as I expect the Arago sails tomorrow.

We have received no pay yet, & I will not try to tell when we will get our pay. Perhaps it will be two months more. Then

MERRY CHRISTMAS

we will have $96 dolls. due in wages and $ 33.33 in bounty due. They can do as they have a mind to.

I am in hopes that war will flag out before our time is out. Evrything looks favourable at present if we suffer no serious disaster.

I have a letter written to J.& J. Conklin and one for J. White. You mentioned in your last that you had received a letter from Margaret, and she said that I did not send my directions. I supposed I did, and can hardly believe to the contrary.

I have mentioned some things I want Geo. Warren to bring for me. I could mention things, but Geo. will be coming back before this reaches you. I have plenty of clothes of all kinds at present. Those stamps come aceptable. I am ashamed to let the mail go north without a letter for Charley & Jim. Net owes me a letter. I have received no letter from J. White since the 22 of last month. Evrybody owes me letters, but I think they mean to.

I shall have to close as I will have to get up twice tonight to go on guard. We need all our sleeping time. Give my love & respects to all. Remember me to my old Mamma-in-Law and all the rest of the folks.

DEAR WIFE

Yours ever and the same,
D.B. White
Co. K 144th

P.S. My head aches some tonight.
You will not see any fotographs until I get some pay. I wish I could send them now, but if I live, they will come someday.

Mrs. Daniel B. White
Downsville, Delaware County, NY

         Hilton Head, SC
        Tuesday, Jan. 31, 1865

Dear Wife,

 I seat myself this morning to pen a few lines to you. I enjoy verry good health at present, and sincerely hope this may find you all enjoying the same blessing.

 First relief to the guard house — that is the order, so I must obey. I will write sometime today. Order countermanded, so I will keep on writing.

MERRY CHRISTMAS

I have no news to write of importance. There has been some changes here since I last wrote to you. There was about 100 men detailed out of the regiment to go to Savannah after a sawmill. They started last Friday night, went to Savannah, and came back Sunday night.

There was about 100 detailed to go north with prisoners. They started last Saturday, taking 6 or 700 prisoners, nearly all the privates that was here under confinement and some officers, but we have 150 in the Provo Yard yet. Where the boys will take them is a matter of mere conjecture. They were to report to Fortress Monroe, and some say that they are going to New York. Others say to Fort Delaware or to Elmira, so I will not try to tell where they have gone.

The boys that went expect to have a fifteen days furlough and go home, but I fear they will be disapointed. There was none detailed from Co. K or D, so none have gone except Ruswell Stevens. He was sent from the Provo Yard. I should [have] liked to go if they go home, otherwise I had rather stay here.

The weather is cold enough here that any person going north as guard will more than freeze. We had a white frost this morning. The ground looked more like winter than any time since I have been here. The weather has been verry cold for the past week, and perhaps we will have another rain storm soon, then another cold snap again.

Col. Lewis would like to have us go back to the regiment and send a detail to do the duty here each day, but I think he will hardly make out to have us removed right away. It would be verry inconvenient for us to do the duty as we would have to carry our knapsacks down here each morning, and 70 men would have to stay where there is only room for 25 and have things convenient, and the Provo Martial alows that he wants one steady guard to do the duty here.

Our Captain alows that he will not take his company back to camp if he can get round doing so, as the Colonel has ordered all our tents taken away. The tents were condemed, and evry board, slab, and post is taken away that belonged to our Co. and Co. D. Our cook house is all removed also, and the Captain says he does not like the style of taking his company there and pitching them in the sand, as cold as the weather is at present, but how they will make it I cannot tell. If the Colonel has more influence with Gen. Foster than the officers of Co. K and D and the Provo Martial, then we will have to go back. Otherwise we will be likely to stay here some time. If our tents were as good as the day we left them, I had rather go back, but as they are now, and nuthing to rebuild them, I had rather stay here until the weather gets warmer.

I have been on guard evry day since I wrote you last, and will be for the next month to come if we get no help. The boys are all getting pretty well tired out, still they keep doing. I fear that many will pay for it when the weather begins to get warm and they have much fatigue, as they will all be about tuckred out and then, look out for sickness.

I will have to go on my post again soon. I stand on the same post that I did when I last wrote, and am getting tired of it, but so long as I am blessed with good health I can get along any place.

I have had a severe cold and cough for the past week, but am getting better now.

I have received no letter from you for some time. The last was dated January 11th. I received one from James dated Jan. 20th. He wrote that he had sold the hay. I wrote to you some time ago to reserve what you wanted to winter your cow or what you have to winter. I do not think I wrote to Jim about reserving any, but I presume you have told him what you wanted as you never mentioned to me whether you wanted any or how much. I think if your folks have taken the sheep that they will need some more hay than they had. I wish I had known about it as it might be some trouble to replace what it would be nesessary to have, and as the hay is, or was, there, it would be better to keep enough for our own use before selling.

Well, I will leave the hay matter as I presume you have atended to it. You never told me whether your folks had taken the sheep or what you have done with them, and how many you sold and how many you have kept.

I suppose you have had a severe winter. So far, how much snow has there been and how much sleighing? And, what is your father and the boys doing?

I will close this letter as I have to leave at present but may have time to write some more this afternoon.

Afternoon

I have just come in off post and eat my dinner, composed of coffee and bread, not a heavy dinner for me with evry day duty, but it is only for 7 months more.

I saw Wm. Johnston yesterday. He is getting quite well again and wants to go to his company again. He is at the hospital yet.

We are having a fine day today. I hope we may have more such.

I have received very few letters for some time past. I wrote to Margaret while she was at Tompkins, also to Cousin Nett, but have received no answer from either. I think it about time that I had another letter from Nett. I wrote to J. Penny a long time ago, but have received no answer yet. Our regiment are generally enjoying good health.

MERRY CHRISTMAS

Buell received two letters from Jane last mail. She mentioned being down to your folkses. She says Mr. Merritt's people are verry kind to her. Buell says he hopes Uncle John will not loose his woman while he is in the army, or he will be likely to lose his woman.

Where is J.W. Stevens? I have heard that he is in York City. Ruswell intends to go and see him if he gets to New York.

James wrote to me to have me tell him what to do with my bounty money. The Supervisor of the Town of Bovina promised me when I took the bond last fall that if I wrote to him requesting him to let it run another year that they would do so. He thought I wrote to him requesting him to let it remain as it was for another year, and received an answer alowing that the Town wished to pay up all bounty moneys, and the money would be left at the National Bank, Delhi to meet the bond. So what to do with the money, I cannot tell. If I was at home myself, I could use it. James said that he thought he could get a bond against the Town of Hamden for the money. Whether to take the bond or not is what troubles me. I am afraid that those bonds will play out, but how soon I cannot tell.

I notice that there has been a bill presented before Congress to prohibit paying local bounties. Whether the bill will pass or go under the table is the question I would like to have answered. I want to put the money in a safe place if possible. It is a hard matter to get money and a hard matter to keep it. Just at the present time it is a hard matter to put money where it would be safe with the present agitation in all kinds of business, and I answered him thus, to do with it as he thought best. He had a better chance to know how matters is at home than I do here, and he will do as well for me as for himself I think. My bounty money is the dearest fought money I ever had in my life, and money that costs me many nights duty and hours of lost time for sleep.

I once thought that I would never send home for money, but I do not know but I shall have to as it is a hard matter to get along without a little and there is no prospect of getting pay. You may send me two or three dolls in a letter, and if that comes safe and I need it, I will send for more if nesesary. Send it if you have it to spare. If not, I will get along. Robert [White: Daniel's nephew] sent me 60 cts. in Jim's letter, and wanted me to have my likeness taken and send it to him, but it takes $1.00 to have a likeness taken, and I had no change to add to it to make the dollar. I promised to send it to him as soon as I could get it taken.

I shall have to close for the present. You must write to me often as it is a great satisfaction to hear from you often. Give my respects to all, remember me to all your folks. Excuse bad writing and spelling, also bad composition, and I remain your true friend and affectionate husband.

D.B. White

Union officers and men at Hilton Head Island.

1864
U.S. Army General Hospital wards, Hilton Head Island.

Regimental Band, Hilton Head Island.

Lt. Col. J. H. Jackson and wife, Hilton Head Island.

Typical enlisted cookhouse, Hilton Head Island.

Officers playing dominoes, Hilton Head Island.

Union veterans of Downsville in the late 1870s.

MERRY CHRISTMAS

After a resounding failure in December of 1864, Fort Fisher, North Carolina was captured by the Union army on January 15, 1865. Naval forces commanded by Admiral David Porter had bombarded the fort for two days when the expeditionary force under Major General Alfred Terry landed on the 15th and captured Fort Fisher. This action partially closed-down the last remaining Confederate blockade running port. On February 22nd, the Union army would capture nearby Wilmington, effectively isolating the Southern armies from supply by the sea.

On January 18th General Sherman turned over command of Savannah to General Foster, and issued orders to begin the march northward through the Carolinas. Sherman's goal was to join forces with Grant for the final push on Petersburg and Richmond.

Sherman would later call the march through Georgia to the sea "child's play" when compared with the logistical problems he faced in moving 60,000 men northward through the marshes and swamps and across the swollen winter-time rivers of the Carolina lowcountry. Confederate leaders thought it couldn't be done.

After some feinting and maneuvering designed to convince the Confederate Generals that he planned to attack Charleston, Sherman's armies began their march on February 1st, bypassing Charleston altogether, and cutting it off from the Confederacy. The Union army headed toward Columbia, the capitol of South Carolina.

DEAR WIFE

Mrs. Daniel B. White
Downsville, Delaware County, NY

Hilton Head, SC
Thursday, Feb. 2, 1865

Dear Wife,

 I seat myself to pen a few more lines to you. I am happy to inform you that I still enjoy verry good health, and my earnest wish is that these lines may find you all enjoying the same blessing.

 I write at present to inform you that our regiment has left Hilton Head once more. They received marching orders night before last and left last night about one o'clock. Where they have gone, we do not know yet. They took ten days rations I believe. We think they have gone up near Savannah to clean out some cavalry that have been making some trouble for our men.

 I suppose that Col. Lewis was verry anxious to have us relieved, but we are not relieved yet, but how soon we may be I cannot tell. Gen. Littlefield sent some Nigers here last night to relieve us, but the Provo Martial would not accept them.

There was men sent from our company and Co. D to relieve the town guard last night, and they are there yet. I cannot tell whether they will be back today or not, but I know we need them here, for we had few enough here before any were taken away.

I will not close this until I hear something from the regiment, unless I have to go after them. In that case, I will inform you by closing this. I think our Col. will whip us nearly all out before the year is ended if he can have his way about keeping us on raids most part of the time. If the Col. gets us back to the regiment again, we need not look for much levity the remainder of our time, but I trust we will come out all right.

Saturday, Feb. 4, 1865

I take my pen once more to write a few lines to you. As for being well today, I am not. Still, I am not very sick. I have had a severe cold for some time and have a head ache. I am excused from duty today, but think I shall be round tomorow again.

I received letters today from James, Margaret, Nett, John, and yourself, and was happy to hear that you were all well.

I cannot tell you for certain where the regiment have gone, but I suppose they have gone on some island near

Charleston. I fear that they will see a rough time. They are assisting Sherman take Charleston. They will do the principal part of the fighting, and Sherman's men will get the praise, as it was at Honey Hill. The men under Foster done the fighting that led to the capture of Savannah, and Sherman received all the praise.

There has been three cases of Small Pox in the regiment that I have heard from, and two deaths. Delos Bates of Co. C is one of the dead. The other I have not heard who or what his name was. I am sorry to hear that the Small Pox has got into the regiment, but I trust it will not spread any more.

You are having fine times sleighriding this winter, well go on. I am glad to hear that you can enjoy life; I only wish I could be with you, but I trust God will spare my life to meet you on earth again. Then we will try to enjoy life once more.

I was sorry to hear that Nett and you could not send me your fotagraphs, but it will be good when it comes. The folks at home I suppose think I might write to them, but when I write to you, and that is so often, I have nuthing to write that would be news after hearing what is in your letters. It would only be a repetition of the same story.

I will write to Charley and Jim as soon as I find anything new that would intrest them. I shall not write to Nett this mail I think, but will soon. She is one of my particular friends, as she has the care of your welfare on her head. She

MERRY CHRISTMAS

thinks you rather unruly sometimes, but I guess I will not say anything about your cutting round at present.

No more at this time. Good by.
D.B. White

Mrs. Daniel B. White
Downsville, Delaware County, NY

> Hilton Head, SC
> Sunday, Feb. 5, 1865

Dear Wife,

I will endeavour to pen a few more lines to you this morning. I am all right again today, and hope this may find you well as I am.

There is no news of importance to write. We hear nuthing from the regiment that is reliable, and I do not know where they are. Neither do I know where the boys have gone that went north. If they get furloughs to go home, you will see Ruswell Stevens. He will be home if any of the boys get furloughs.

DEAR WIFE

I shall have to report to the Sergeant of the Guard. I will write some more today if I get time.

Afternoon

30 men detailed out of Co. K with ten days rations. I will mail this before going. I will write soon if I have a chance.

Yours in haste,
D.B. White

If Jane hears nuthing from Buell, tell her that he told me to ask you to tell her that he is detailed with the crowd.

Monday, Feb. 6, 1865

Great cry and little wool! I am in my quarters, tent No. 6, this morning. Am well; what greater blessing could I ask.

Our excitement of yesterday has died away in a measure, and the boys are still in the Provo Yard, but we are not certain whether those that were detailed yesterday afternoon will go away or stay here. There was some packing knapsacks in a hurry yesterday after they detailed and asorted. I was chosen as one of the number that should stay here. Buell is among the number that goes, if any go. They are detailed to go on board iron side boats to do duty there. Perhaps if they go they will have a good time and easy duty. It is supposed that Charleston or some of the islands near that place will be the field for the boats to operate in, and men that go may have a pleasant time, and they may have a rough time. I will write more about this matter hereafter.

The Provo Martial, I suppose, raised cain last night when he was informed that these road men [were] called for from our company and Co. D, and he has been working ever since to have the order countermanded. He alows that he has these two companies in his charge, and he does not wish to have them taken away and others sent here to do duty here. He has been our friend in several cases, and the boys will do anything for him that he chooses to ask for within the bonds of reason. Today will tell whether his influence will keep the boys here or not.

The Arago arived this morning, and George Warren came here aboard of her. The mail will be sorted so we will get it tonight, but I do not look for any this mail.

There is one thing I would lecture you about. You have mentioned ocasionally about buying articles of dress. Well that is alright, but you have spoken in such a manner that I take it that you seem to think that I will think you extravigant or that you buy things not nesesary. Now, I would rather not hear anything more about that. I want you to get what you need or think you need, and alow that I may be suited with your style or otherwise, and when I complain, then it will be time enough to plead nesesity. Be independent as long as you can, then when you cannot swim, sink.

Tuesday evening, Feb. 7, 1865

I will endeavour to pen a few more lines to you. I am still in a state of verry good health.

I will inform of the fact that 30 from our company left the Yard this afternoon about 4 o'clock to go aboard a gun boat, and there was 30 men taken from Co. D, and that leaves us in a position that we have to go on post 12 hours out of 24 or half the time, on two hours and off two.

I have been kept busy for the past week. A few days before the call came for the boys that have gone, the Captain came to the guard house and told the boys that there was two posts, one in front of the Provo Martial's, where I wrote to you that I had been so long, and one other where officers passed into and out of the Provo Yard. Well now, I will tell you what he said about the two posts. He said that any four men that would clean his [their] gun and straps and equipage the best would be posted on them posts and be relieved evry other day. That was to be the reward for cleaning accouterments well. I got the post in front of the Martial's the first day, but the raid knocked the thing all in the head before I realized the benefits of the position then. I have a squad of 10 or 12 men now, (there was 15 before the boys left) that I had to

MERRY CHRISTMAS

atend to and see that they keep all their things in order and tent clean, the rooms have to be scrubbed two or three times each week..

Well now, I think I have written about all I know that would be news to you. Buell has written to Jane today. If you see her and she is alarmed about him, tell her that the boys that have gone think they will have a good time. I hope they will, but cannot tell how it will turn out.

You must tell all your folks that I have no news other than I have written, and it would be a waste of time and paper to write to any of them at present.

I have heard that the regiment is on Johns Island doing guard duty there. I guess you will not see me to Elmira verry soon.

James wrote that I would be likely to have a visit from you. Would to God I could have your company for 24 hours if it could not be any longer time.

There has no officers gone with the boys except two Corporals from each company. We have had a cold wet storm for a few days past.

Be shure and write soon, and direct as before. I cannot tell whether we will stay here long, but letters will follow us. If this reaches you before you send any money, I would

DEAR WIFE

rather you would mail the letter with the money in Delhi or Hamden Post Office, as I think I have never lost any letters mailed at either Hamden or Delhi, but if you cannot send the letter to either place handily, put it in the office at Downsville.

I will write again soon. Excuse this miserable letter, and I will try to do better next time.

From your ever true friend.
D.B. White

CHAPTER FIVE

THE DESERTERS

Mrs. Daniel B. White
Downsville, Delaware County, NY

Hilton Head, SC
Monday, Feb. 13, 1865

Dear Wife,

I take the present opurtunity to pen a few more lines to you. I am happy to inform you that I enjoy good health, & I sincerely hope this may find you all enjoying the same blessing.

I received a letter from you last night dated February 1st, & I was pleased to hear that you were all enjoying good health. It is a great pleasure to hear from you often, and I am disappointed when the mail comes without a letter.

DEAR WIFE

You alowed that George mailed a letter to me at the same time you did the one that you calculated to send with Geo. Warren. I have not received that letter yet and perhaps never will. Tell him to write another, and I think it will come to hand.

I think you was somewhat roiled and felt a little rough towards Jane, but I guess it will be hardly worth your while to resent a statement made by her, as I conclude that it will make but little or no difference to either you or I. Still I glory in your spunk, and would rather see you resent any false statements than to alow any person to infringe on your rights or priveledges without letting the person, whoomsoever he or she may be, know that you are capable of doing your own business and atending to it. As for your having a man that is capable of wearing the breeches, we will settle that matter if we both live to meet again. God grant that we may be priviledged to see that happy day when peace may again smile on our once happy, but now distracted, country.

I think that Nett and Charley is cutting round considerable this winter. You alow that you do not enjoy yourself in company. Perhaps it is not human nature that you should enjoy yourself in company as you once did, but I am pleased to hear that you go and make our friends a social visit. I wish you to enjoy yourself as best you can. I think if I were in your place, I should want to cut round some to kill time, for I am shure it must be lonesome times in Delaware County at the present time.

THE DESERTERS

I received a letter from James a few days since, dated February 1st, and he said that he was going over to the hollow, and was going to try hard to have you go home with him to stay a while. If you were in the clove, and I was shure of it, I would direct this to Hamden, but I think I shall direct it to Downsville as usual, then you will get it sometime, no doubt.

I think John and Jane Conklin does not calculate to answer the last letter I wrote to them.

You have had a call from J. Penny and wife and son. Well I'll bet you had a lively time while they were there. I presume Jim told all he knew, perhaps more. If you see him again and he still alows that I have any right to that youngster, just tell him to send it home as soon as it is weaned, and that will make a commensement for me.

I think Rob wades in pretty fast for a boy, don't you, and Tom Scott, he is tough as tripe. There will be a scene there again perhaps.

How is Nance Aaron?, show out about this time perhaps.

Well I guess I am writing a rough letter, in case this letter should fall in strange hands. I should like to be home a while to spark the girls a little again. I get tired sparking wenches, and a change would be lightsome.

DEAR WIFE

You alow that Hat Sackett sent her respects to me. Well when you see her again you can tell her that if John can't spark her often enough, just wait until I get home, then I will make a visit. Tell her that I shall not forget her if John does, but I presume there is no danger. He is just like a little bull pup, the more he runs round, the more he wants to. I will put a split stitch on his tail, and then we will see whether he will run over to Sackett Harbour or after Mary Hulbert either. If he should see this, he would be after my sweet life I presume, but I don't care. I am in South Carolina and safe as far as he is concerned.

Ed White is in the company and made a discovery a few days ago. I mentioned our having six Reb officers in confinement with a special guard to atend to them for stripping one of their officers for supposed Union sentiments. They have a room done off in a chamber where refugees stay. Well Ed has been guarding those men, and has a fair chance to see all the refugees that are in the yard as he is outside of the room where the Rebs stay, and among the refugees he discovered a man among the refugees or Reb deserters last Thursday that he alowed was John Bogart, brother to Ace and Ed. He was a member of the 8th NY Battery at one time, and deserted [June 12, 1862], but where he was no one knew for certain, but we know that he deserted and was in the Reb Army.

How he came there still remains to be seen, but to return to my story, as I have said, Ed noticed him , and told some of the boys that if John Bogart was not among that crowd of refugees, he never knew him. That put the boys on the alert, and Ed gave us a discription of the man he called Bogart. He was dressed in Reb pants and jacket and cap with a black broadcloth coat. I presume Bogart smelt the rat and knew Ed, and Ed enquired some into his former residence, Bogart claiming that his name was Davis and he was born and brought up in Virginia.

He kept out of the way until yesterday morning. James Scott having charge of the refugees rations, he discovered him when he came to draw his rations, and he claimed that the man that represented himself to be Davis was no more or less than John Bogart. Someone informed Capt. Griffith that there was a man there that they suspected to be different from what he represented himself to be.

Cap. came and called Corp. Warren and went to the refugee room and found him and ordered him to appear before the Martial. Then [Thomas] Pine and several of the boys that used to be acquainted with John went to the Provo Martial's. John saw that he was recognized and owned up and is under lock and key. How it will go with him I am not able to say, but the general opinion is that he will swing for desertion. Such is often the penalty of desertion from our country in her time of trial.

When the boys saw him and he knew that he was recognized, he knew several of the boys good. Will hear more from him before long. His calculation was to swing clear under the asumed name of Davis and be sent to New York among the other Reb deserters.

Daniel Smith received notice last night of the death of his eldest son. Tough news for a soldier and so far from home with no chance to be with afflicted friends at home.

There is a report that our regiment has been in battle again, and lost some men, but there is nuthing reliable as to the confirmation of the report as yet.

How is it with you concerning shoes? You have never mentioned getting any new ones, and I am shure you must have got a new pair or you would need them. I presume you are aware that I had some sole leather in my chest, and I guess you had better have James cut you off a pair sometime when you are up the clove if you need them. I hope you will not wear shoes that leak and keep your feet wet. If you can aford to, buy you new ones.

You mentioned in your last letter that you calculated to send me some money by express. As the matter stands at present, I cannot tell whether to expect any to come by express if you rec. my last [letter] before you express any, as I alowed that you might send me two or three dollars in a letter and run the risk of getting it. I can get along without money I suppose, but a little better with a few dollars as I am not certain when we may receive any pay.

THE DESERTERS

We will soon have $130 dollars due us, but we may not get it in some time yet. I always thought I never should have any money come from home to me while in the service, but I should not refuse it at present should it come. I received $3.00 in James' last letter. I would not be any alarmed about money sent in a letter from Hamden, but I lose so many letters mailed at Downsville; I cannot tell the reason why it is so.

Tuesday, Feb. 14, 1865

I once more take my pen in hand to scribble a few more lines to you. I am well today, and it is raining. We have had some cold weather, and I presume the wind blows as hard here sometimes as it has in Delaware County, and the sand flies as thick and fast as the snow there, and often get my eyes, ears and mouth full. I grate my teeth and bear it.

You alow that I am not well or chew too much tobacco. I am well and have been most part of the time since I left home, and as to the tobacco, I think I have not chewed over one pound in any week since I came to Hilton Head. I think I know what ails me. I do not get any whiskey. Our noncommissioned, and I might add commissioned, officers drink all the whiskey, and you know it was as natural to me as my mother's milk, and that's what's the matter. If I had some cider and molasses I would fat up in a short time.

I would be as rich as Tom White alowed he was the other night. He said he was worth $5,000 at night, and next morning he was not worth d____d a dollar in the Lord's world. I received notice in my last letter from James that he loaned to Town of Hamden $800 dolls. and had the intrest in his hands amounting to about $28.00.

Now I will tell you about the fire they had downtown this morning. A fire broke out about 4 o'clock and destroyed two houses. One I believe belonged to Capt. Pratt and the other to an Ordnance Sargeant, and the Ordnance Department came near being burned, but with the asistance of men and three engines the flames were extinguished, a happy termination. If the fire had fairly got going in the Ordnance stores among powder and shell, I think there would have been some broken heads and lost property. They have arested two clerks on suspicion that have been clerks in town for some time.

I think I shall have to close this letter; I have sometimes thought I should burn it, as it is rather rough and somewhat smuty, but I shall mail it and let it bring what it is worth.

Goodbye for the present. Your ever true friend and sincere husband.

D.B. White

THE DESERTERS

P.S. If you wish to put any extras on my letters, or .think they will come safer

Direct:	Daniel B. White
Co. K, 144th Regt. N.Y.S.V.
Hilton Head, SC   C/O: Capt. J. Rich

Mrs. Daniel B. White
Downsville, Delaware County, NY

Hilton Head, SC
Wednesday, February 15, 1865

Dearest Companion,

I presume you will think that my store of writing matter must be nearly run out, but I think I can convince you to the contrary by writing a large sheet full evry day. I received one more letter from you this morning. Don't you believe that I was happy to hear from you again. I'll bet I was, and you may follow the bet and be sure to win too.

I am verry well today, with the exception of a severe headache caused by having a heavy cold which I have had for the past month. You seem to borrow a good deal of trouble about my health, and think it would be a fine thing to try to get a substitute. Perhaps it might be. Don't you recolect a piece in the old school reader headed, "Is not God upon the Water as well as on the Land". Now, my dear friend, cannot God protect me in the army as well as in Delaware County? Think of this dearest companion, and thank Him for bestowing the blessing of health on me and you and our friends that are near and dear to us, with the blessings of home and kind friends to you.

Just look over the broad field of misery and desolation that this war has caused, the fathers, husbands, and brothers and sons that have been lost to friends forever on earth, and then I would ask you whether you have cause to complain. You have never laid down to sleep troubling with the fear that you might lose friends, house and home, and perhaps dear life by some ruthless hand before the closing of another day. How many have felt that such might be their fate.

Now the question arises, and I will answer it. Will I hire a substitute, I think not. In the first place it might, and no doubt would be, a hard matter to get one, then ten chances to one whether I could arrange matters so I could have him take my place and I be sent home, that dearest spot on earth. Secondly, alow that I had a substitute hired, and then how long would it take to get papers from the War Department before I could start for home with things all working to my satisfaction. I could not hope to get things arranged in less than two or three months, perhaps four, and probably five. Then what would it profit me. My time would be most out.

Thirdly, should I leave the friends of my youthful days to do battle with my enemies as well as theirs, and desert them to enjoy the comforts of home, they to endure the hard life of a soldier. Some of them have lain on the cold, damp earth and in many other uncomfortable places for two years and one half and for only six months with as comfortable quarters as the boys were ever in.

I agree with you money is no object to me contrasting it with a soldier's life. Still, I feel much more contented when I think you will not be likely to suffer from want. You have my answer, and may it please God to spare our lives to meet on earth once more, is my earnest wish.

I will bid you good-by for the present, and inform you that a boat came down from the place where the regiment has been on James Island, and brought sixteen wounded and reported one killed when the boat left. I have heard it reported since that the regiment left the island, finding it too warm for them, and was on transports out in Bull's Bay. Perhaps I shall hear more from them before closing.

I understand that the Reb prisoners have been told this afternoon that they are to be exchanged in a few days, and they have been cheering since I seated myself to write, so I conclude it is true.

DEAR WIFE

Thursday, February 16, 1865

I am going to bother your time a little reading some more of my nonsense. I am well today with the exception of my old fashioned headache. You seem to think I have lost a good deal of flesh since leaving home, but I must add that I have been gaining some lately. I will try to find time to go to town tomorrow, and I shall be weighed again. That will tell the story. The mail may close tomorrow, but I think not.

Friday, February 17, 1865

All right today except my evryday headache. Nuthing new. Just came from town; bought a newspaper; am going to send it home. Was weighed; net weight without overcoat, 146 lbs. I guess you will have to give up the idea of outweighing me. No more at present. Be shure to write often.

Your ever true friend,
D.B. White

Saturday, February 18, 1865

Philo Allison taken to General Hospital. Has been sick 3 or 4 days.

[The following letter to Amanda's young brother, James Merritt, was enclosed]

THE DESERTERS

Thursday, February 16, 1865

Friend James,

I received your letter dated February 8th, and will try to write a few lines in answer.

You say that you are going to school and have a good teacher. I am glad to hear that you have a chance to atend school. I will give you some advice that I should have taken years ago. Never think you cheat the teacher by making believe you have a lesson when you have not. You may cheat a teacher, but it does not injure the teacher half so much as it will you. If you live, you will see days when you will regret the lost time and neglected lessons.

You wrote that Nett and Charley were off to a party when you was writing. Don't you think they run round a good deal. Just tell them I think they are rather unsteady.

You did not tell me that you had the best pair of cattle in the Town, but I supposed you would.

I have no news to write at present. I have written all the news to Amanda.

Do you play dominoes as much this winter as last? I play a game ocasionally, but do not have as much time to spare as when at home. We have had three inspections this week already. That keeps us busy our spare time.

You must write again soon. I am happy to see that you improve finely in writing this winter. I shall have to close for the present. My respects, and I remain your true friend,

D.B. White

Mrs. Daniel B. White
Downsville, Delaware County, NY

Hilton Head, SC
Thursday, Feb. 23, 1865

Dear Wife,

I seat myself once more to pen a few lines to you. I feel happy and contented this morning because I am well and had a letter from you yesterday informing me that you and my friends were all well.

I received a letter from D. and Mag Frasier, also one from J. McLarren and one from J. White. Jim said that Mother & Robert had been off the hooks some but were better when he wrote. Meg Frasier comensed writing her letter January 22nd and closed it February 13th. She avows that she cannot find time to write, and I presume she is kept busy. Yours was dated Feb. 16th.

Well now, for something to write that will be news to you-I might write and tell you that Savannah, Fort Fisher near Wilmington, Charleston, Branchville, and Orangeburg have fallen and is ours, all within the past two months. You would tell me that all this is not news to you. I need not tell you about the regiment unless I say that they have not come back, and we do not know where they are.

I can tell you that the boys that went north came back last Tuesday, and it is reported that they are going again with the rest of the prisoners. I will inform you that there was 20 men detailed from Co. D & K, and started last Monday morning with three days rations and came back last night . They had been up the South Edisto River on a raid, burned some buildings, confiscated some property, and came back all safe. They say that they found one as fine a house and furniture as any of them ever saw. They took what suited their fancy, books, trinkets, furniture, but think the house was not destroyed. They say that the night they were there they could see fires in evry direction, buildings burning. What a destruction of property this war is causing.

You tell me that you sent me some things in a box that More's people were sending to Jonas and Enos. I do not know, but I presume they are both with the regiment.

DEAR WIFE

I think you would all rob yourselves to send things to me. It is a great pleasure to me to think I have friends so kind, still I would rather have you would all keep your things than to sacrifice nesesries to send to me. I am shure that your folks need all the butter they can possibly make. I have bought 4 lbs. of butter since I used up what Nelly & Esther sent to me, and have nearly 2 lbs. left yet. We get splendid butter for 75¢ per lb.. How can I ever repay my friends for their kindness to me.

You stated that you had sent me $10.00 by express. David Minor just came from the Express Office, and says the money is there. I shall have to get an order from the Captain and go after it sometime today. I think Baker took considerable advantage charging $2.00 for expressing it. He took more than $1.50 for his trouble.

I think I shall have a dozen fotagraphs taken soon to send home.

I shall have to close writing soon for I have two more letters to write, and the mail closes today. There is nuthing more to write, and I shall shorten this letter and write soon again.

You stated that you had received no letter from me for two mails. I was shure there would be none one mail on acount of the boat lying here one day over her time. I presume you have received all that I wrote, since you wrote your last to me.

You mentioned that you thought of going to Geo. Fuller's for a week, and alowed that you did not know what you would do next summer. Now I will tell you what I think you had better do, providing Nett is not going to stay at home. If she is from home, you had better stay and help your mother if she needs you and wants you to. I hate the idea of your hireing out for all the difference it will make, after we consider the difference it would make with clothing. Perhaps some may think me too proud to be poor, or rather so proud I always will be poor, but I don't care much what people call me if they don't call me late to dinner.

I intended to write to John and Charley this mail, and will if I can find time. Tell them that I send my best respects to them all; give my love to our kind parents. Remember Nett; tell her to write.

Now I shall inform you of the death of Philo Allison. He was taken with a severe pain in his side, and was sick some two or three days when he was taken to the hospital. We did not suppose him dangerous. Then he went from here last Saturday morning and died Tuesday night about 11 o'clock and was burried yesterday morning. Such is the frailty of man. Life is uncertain; death is inevitable.

DEAR WIFE

I shall close for the present by bidding you good by. May kind heaven protect the dear friends that we love, and the Stars and Stripes float over the land of the free and the home of the brave.

From your most sincere friend and husband,
   D.B. White
   Co. K, 144th Regt.
   Hilton Head, SC
To: A.M. White

P.S. What do you think about me joining the Regular Army and making soldiering my business for life? If you think it would be advisable, let me know soon.

Mr. Charles Merritt
Downsville, Delaware County, NY

        Hilton Head, SC
       Saturday, February 25, 1865

Friend Charles,

It is with pleasure that I take my pen in hand to write a few lines to you. I received a letter from you so long time ago. I was pleased to hear from you, but thought you would excuse me for the reason that I was writing so often to Amanda, and was shure that you would learn all that was news from me and concerning the movements of the 144th NYSV.

I had written to Amanda and mailed the letter two days ago, but think it has not gone north because the mail boat is here yet and will sail tomorrow. I have written to John, and shall send this in the same envelope.

As for news, I cannot write any. I will surely state that there is a report here to night that Wilmington has fallen into our hands, but we have none of the particulars.

You can tell Amanda that I have learned today that Enos & Jonas More is at camp, and one of them is in the Regimental Hospital, but do not know which of the two.

The box did not come on the Arago, but will be here when the Fulton comes, and that will be in 4 or 5 days. Then I look for some letters from home again. Amanda says she did not receive any mail for two mails, but I wrote as usual.

Tell Amanda and Nett that I was downtown this morning and sat for photographs and was down this evening and saw about how they were taken. They were pretty good, but the artist thought he could better them, and I shall go down tomorrow or next day and try again if I have my health and nuthing happens to prevent.

Sergt. W.R. Stevens was at New York and saw Wesley. He thinks he will have to have to lose his leg, but he is comfortable and has the best of care.

Amanda tells me that you and Nett goes to lots of parties this winter, and I hope you are enjoying yourself and wish I was home to go with you sometimes, don't you, but I think I shall be with you again soon. Trusting that it may be so, I will bid you good bye for the present. Don't forget to write, if I neglect to answer your letter. It is a great pleasure to hear from you all, and often.

My respects to all, and I remain your true friend and well wisher,

Daniel B. White

P.S. If you was here one week you would hear better music than you ever heard in Delaware County. We have good musicians and lots of musical instruments, but money and whiskey is high, so high we don't often reach either. The whiskey is of little acount, and my friends have been so kind as to send me a little money.

Daniel's assertion on February 4th that "the men under Foster done the fighting that led to the capture of Savannah, and Sherman received all the praise" is simply incorrect.

THE DESERTERS

Foster's men were only engaged in trying to break the Charleston and Savannah Railroad, not with the actual push on Savannah. The Honey Hill action did draw Confederate troops away from Savannah at a critical time, but that small number of soldiers would not have made a difference in General Hardee's decision to evacuate the city.

The Confederacy was unable to assemble a force large enough to counter Sherman's onslaught. As Sherman's men marched northward through South Carolina in early February, Hardee was at Charleston, General Beauregard in Columbia. Both were trying to slow Sherman's progress through the use of harassing actions on Sherman's columns and by burning bridges and blocking roads in his path. Both knew they did not have the manpower to stand and fight.

Sherman reached Columbia on February 16th, and as his men began to surround the city, General Beauregard withdrew; he could not prevent the city's capture. On the morning of the 17th, Columbia's mayor surrendered, and sometime that night the city was set ablaze. Historians differ in their assessment of who actually started the fires, Sherman's men or the retreating Confederate forces, but the city burned for days, and much of it was destroyed.

At the same time Columbia was being surrendered to Union forces, General Hardee was evacuating Charleston. Again, he knew he could not prevent the city's capture. He took what war materiel he could, and withdrew toward the north.

February 17, 1865 was a sad day for the Confederacy. Columbia and Charleston, "the birthplace of secession", had fallen. Sherman's devastating and demoralizing march went unchecked.

DEAR WIFE

On the 22nd Wilmington, North Carolina was captured. General Braxton Bragg wisely withdrew, taking what stores and war materiel he could.

Sherman's 60,000 troops were pushing the smaller Confederate armies before them and leaving devastation in their wake. The "march to the sea" is remembered, but the march northward through South Carolina was worse. Sherman's men were taking their revenge on the cradle of secession, and Sherman did little to control them.

Mrs. Daniel B. White
Downsville, Delaware County, NY

Hilton Head, SC
Wednesday, March 1, 1865

Dear Wife,

I now seat myself to pen a few more lines to you. I am happy to inform you that I am well, and sincerely hope these lines may find you all as well as it leaves me. I received a long letter from you yesterday dated February 26 and 28. You cannot imagine how much comfort it is to hear from you and to hear that you are all well.

We are running this Provo Yard in our own style now days. The prisoners have all left. They were sent north. I

THE DESERTERS

believe I mentioned to you in my last [letter] that there had been a detail of 100 men from the regiment to go with them as guards. None from our company went except our 1st Lieutenant, C.M. Hathaway.

I saw George Hawk yesterday. He had just returned from where our regiment was, about 60 miles out into the country from Charleston. There was several that came back with him to Charleston, and some came back to camp. George said that he understood them to say that all the boys were coming back in a few days. He thought they were near Charleston when he left yesterday. He saw the boys on the boats, and alowed that they were getting along finely.

It is reported here and generally believed that the 144th have been ordered back here to do the guard duty, and that we are detached. Still, I think there is nuthing verry certain about it. I do not know, neither do I care much whether we stay here our time out or go somewhere else. There is one thing. If we stay we will not have long marches and we have comfortable quarters. When we are on guard and it is raining we have good sentry boxes to stand in and do not get much wet.

I fear that you are rather discontented from what you write, and count on chickens before they are hatched. I hope sincerely and truly that we may both be spared by the hand of kind Providence to meet and enjoy all the pleasure you picture out in fancy, but dear friend, remember the parable of the rich man who said, "Soul, be of good cheer, thou hast riches laid up for many years". Also remember the injunction, "This night thy soul shall be required of thee". Life is uncertain; death inevitable, but I leave that subject hoping that you have seen the falicy of trusting in your own strength or that of mankind. May the ruler of the universe be pleased in His all wise and just dealings with us, be pleased to spare our lives to meet once again and enjoy each others company and bear each others burdens through the rugged paths of life, is the earnest wish of your best and truest friend on earth, D.B.W.

Saturday, Mar. 4, 1865

I cannot write much today as I am on guard and shall have to go to the guard house soon, but tomorow is Sunday, and if I have my health, I shall have time to write. I am on guard evry other day for four days, then I am off two days in succesion. Our duty is light at present. How soon they may make changes I cannot say.

You speak of being in Loyd's Clove visiting. I presume you have had a lively time for it is a noble place to go visiting.

I received a letter from J. & J. Conklin yesterday. They were rather short winded. Still I am happy to receive short letters rather than none at all. I shall have to write a pretty rough letter to Jane next time. I think she might take things more cool in war times. Silk dresses and fancy bonnets are beyond the pictures in war times.

You shall have to look sharp if you make out to read all the cross hoppled words I have written.

D.B. White

Mrs. Daniel B. White
Downsville, Delaware County, NY

Hilton Head, SC
Sunday, March 12, 1865

Dear Companion,

I will atempt to write a few more lines to you today. I can hardly settle my mind to think of anything this morning. I have had an old fashioned headache all night, but after stirring round and eating a little breakfast, I feel a considerable better. You need not trouble yourself about my having the headache. I shall get over that when I get rid of the cold I have had for the past two months.

The weather is comfortably warm here now. We have had a considerable [amount] of rain and cloudy weather, but not cold for the past month. If I had any news to write, I could get along better than I am likely to as it is.

I received a letter from James a few days ago. He said he had not been in the hollow for some time, but intended to go soon. He said John McLarren had collected a debt I had standing against John McKee of $18.00 and a few cents, and that he had in his hands at that time a few cents over $28.00, and that if you did not need it, he would use it until spring. I requested him some time since to give Mother $5.00. I thought it my duty to give her a little money to use as she choosed to. She has done lots of work for me that she had never received pay for.

I want to know whether you have what you need before any person has any by my concent. If so, then I would as lief Jim would have it as anyone. He alows he will pay the interest as long as he uses it. I do not know how much money [you] have or how much you have had, neither do I care, as long as you have what you want to use, for I see no trouble about you spending any foolishly. I hope to get pay soon, and if I do and get what is due me, I think I can send $100.00 home.

We are looking for the regiment evry day. The boys in Company K are all getting along as well as can be expected. Some few are sick with colds, but they are all round ocasionaly. Corneal Bennett was taken sick the first part of last week, and had a breaking out all over him. We were afraid first that it was Small Pox, but the Doctor, when he came to see him, thought it was the Measles. He is in the General Hospital.

I think John could hardly better himself if he can get $400.00 for one year and a good place to work, pay shure, &c.

Have you received the letters I sent last mail, one directed to you and one to Nett with two fotagraphs in each. I sent a book also.

You mentioned something about working out, and supposed it would suit me as well if you did not. That last asersion is as near the truth as you will be likely to get.

You say those shoes I had made for you was worth half a dozen pairs of (sail) shoes. The next time you buy, get a pair made in shop or buy sale shoes. I don't like those (sail) shoes you have been in the habbit of wearing.

You think I was mistaken about not receiving a letter from George. It is possible, I may be, but if so I have been labouring under a mistake for some time. I looked over what letters I have on hand this morning, but do not find it there. If I cannot make George believe I wrote last, I shall write to him soon.

I expect Tina will be looking for me to send my fotagraph. Perhaps I shall, but I only have three left, and someone will have to be disappointed.

I shall have to close for the present. You are aware that I received a letter from Jane Robinson. I am shure of it, because you directed the letter. She wanted me to try to send a box to him [Buell] that his folks sent. If I could not, she wanted me to open the box and see what was in it and use at least all that would not keep. You can tell her for me that the box has been here three weeks or more, and that I have enquired about his letters, and they have been sent, but the Orderly of the company says he cannot manage to send the Express boxes to the boys. Several have boxes here that are on the boat. I wrote a letter to Buell last week, and expect to hear from him soon, as Sergt. [Frank J.] Campbell went to Charleston last night. I have not opened the box, neither do I feel inclined to do so.

D.B. White

I went up to camp last Tuesday and got the things that were sent from home. I received dried apples, dried beef, shugar, and butter. I guess evrything came all right.

Enos is with the regiment, and Jonas has been in the Regimental Hospital, and I presume is yet. He was up to his tent in his company when I was there. He had lost his speech, and could not speak louder than a whisper, but he will get over that impediment when he gets rid of a bad cold. John Smith was as bad as Jonas, and he could talk nearly as well as ever.

THE DESERTERS

I am going to tell you what one member of Co. K did last Sunday morning. Well he did just what would be hard for you to guess. He simply commited an act entitled an act of matrimony. His name is James Elderkin. His folks live in the Town of Franklin. The woman is a refugee and comes to the Provo Yard and draws her rations. She has been married three or four times before, and has a son some 5 or 6 years old. Don't you think he done a big thing, just as though there was not better women North than any of those refugees are likely to be. I shall not tell you what I think about Southron women, only that I believe them generally to be as kind to strangers as they are honest to their own husbands or lovers.

I wish I could be at home for one night, if no longer, just when you would have a batch of [maple] shugar ready to eat. I think I might eat a little. Well, I won't be there, so you can save me a little hunk and I will thank you for it most kindly, and when it comes as near strawberry time, I hope we will be able to talk about gathering them, but I guess I shall be home to do all the harvesting I shall have to do.

You thought Nett White would write to you. So did I, but she has not, or I have not received it. I changed my corespondents. I wrote to Mary last mail. She will write to me I am shure.

Do you think Nelly will be disapointed because you have not been there this winter? She may be. She wrote to me a long time ago that she thought you would come there and stay a long while this winter, and the last letter she wrote she said David was going over in Huntley Hollow, and she was making calculations for you to acompany him home.

I will close and leave a little space. If the mail does not close tonight, there may be something new to write tomorrow. You must give all the folks at home my love and best respects, and be shure to write. I don't want you to miss one mail, for I never have yet. I have writen a letter evry week since I came on the island.

I am shure you will have a job to read this would be letter. I must twit you a little about your last letter, and you will find room in this to return the compliment. You directed your last [letter] to me and Cair of Capt. J. Rich. I would write <u>care</u> of Capt. J. Rich.

From your dearest and best friend, to a respected wife,
From,
D.B. White

Monday, March 13, 1865

I am feeling noble today. Some of the boys that were on the boat came back to the company last night. Buell did not come. We expect them all back in a few days, also what are with the Colonel.

Yours in haste,
D.B. White

THE DESERTERS

Mrs. Daniel B. White
Downsville, Delaware County, NY

Hilton Head, SC
Monday, March 27, 1865

Dear Wife,

I now seat myself once more to pen a few lines to you. I pass my happiest moments in reading letters from you and writing to you. I am happy to be able to inform you that I am verry well indeed. I sincerely hope you are enjoying as good health as I am at the present time.

I must tell you some good news. I received five letters from old Delaware County this morning, and they all contained some good news for me, altho none were of a verry late date. I received none when the mail came before except the one I received from Sarah [Amanda's sister]. I have written several letters that had not reached home when you wrote the one I received this morning, but I have mentioned all to you that I had written letters to. I wrote one to Tina & George after the mail had left, but did not know it until after I had commensed writing, so I concluded to finish it & mail it.

I will tell you who I received letters from this morning: Mary C. White, John A. McLarren, James P. White, Nett Merritt, & yourself. I wrote to Mary White and sent her my fotograph at the same time. I sent two in a letter to you & two in a letter to Nett. I sent two in a letter to J. White, and they had received them.

Mother sent me many thanks for it, also for the money I gave her. Could I be better repaid for it. She has been a good mother to me. Who would have taken the same care of my clothes that she did when I had no one else to do it for me. Where could I have made myself at home as I did there. Thank God I have another guardian angel added to the list, one near & dear to me as my own life. Yes, I have more than you dearest friend, for I verily believe your parents, your brothers & sisters, I hope all of them, I know some of them, are added to my chain of kindred souls.

If you knew the pleasure I had in reading Nett's letter, you would shurely say she has possession of most kindly feelings in my heart. Esther wrote a few lines to me. She too cannot be otherwise than friendly to me. You may think I have forgotten that people might be deceptive. I have not forgotten that, but I have often heard people say the best way to prove friendship is to seperate. The best way to retain friends is not to be too familiar. Secrets are best kept when kept within our own breasts.

You perhaps want to know if there is anything new at Hilton Head. There is nuthing new, the same scene enacted over & over again. The boys that went north have returned and been home. About 15 men from our Company are on the

THE DESERTERS

boat at Charleston yet. I have not heard from Buell for a few days, but I think he is well. I had a letter from him a short time since. You can tell Jane that his box has been sent to him.

Report only goes to confirm the old report about the Colonel, but in the first place I want you to understand that I would say nuthing against him. We were playmates in childhood; I think he would befriend me now. I cannot vouch for the truth of the asertions I am going to make, as it only comes to me as report. I believe the Colonel is a noble & brave officer, a man of good morals, & a worthy example is set before us by him. Still we do not seem to think alike concerning our Company. He says Co. D & K have had an easy time since they came to the Provo Yard, Co. E likewise. They are in the fort. I heard that he said we had an easy time of it while the rest of the regiment had been marching & fiting, & now he would have us back to camp if it cost him $100.00 or otherwise he would have us all in front of Petersburg in less than six weeks.

There has been plotting & counterplotting between the officers at camp and ours at the Provo Office. This has been going on for the past three months, each party becoming more & more embittered. How it will end remains to be seen, but I fear that it will be of no advantage to us if we join the regiment again. We may expect to toe in then.

DEAR WIFE

It is dinner time, but I am not hungry so I will wait awhile before eating. James writes to me that Hamden has been drafted. John McLarren writes that he is among the drafted. They think it will come out all right yet as the town has hired the men & had them sworn in & paid them. It will be a sad mistake if they lose both men & money.

You all speak of the sickness of R. Christie. I think he has been quite sick, but I hope he will be better by this time.

Esther says you have forgotten them or could not get over to see them. James informs me of the death of one of J. Nichol's children, also of the birth of another at David's. He does not speak of sex. That beats the d____l don't it. I would like to know how many they spoke for.

You had a fine visit in Loyd's Clove, and just called where I should have made the longest stay had I been there, but I shall write to Jane for all that. You were keeping house for Jane; good business for you I presume. Charley has business keeping those grass widows in orders. I cannot say but that I think you will have a verry nice dress, but if you had what I came near saying when I first saw it, you would be surprised some perhaps.

You seem to think I had ought to be cowhided for thinking of such a thing as re-enlisting, but I think I take more comfort here than I would at home with a draft continualy at my heels. The company of those dear friends I have left behind me is the greatest deprivation.

I am glad John apreciated the advice I gave him. I shall stop & eat dinner now. Good by for the present.

Tuesday, March 28, 1865

I take my pen once more to write a few lines. I am on duty today. I wrote an answer for each letter I received except finishing this.

I was up to the old camp last night awhile & saw several of the boys, but saw none that had been home to hear news from home. I do not go to camp often. It is a lonesome place for me. I hope I shall never have to go back there to stay long at a time. We have a great many liberties here that they are deprived of there. I saw Wm. Johnston; he is well. Some of our boys were detailed yesterday to go with men to different places.

I shall have to close for the present. Give my love to all and retain a goodly share for yourself. I wish I could see Erm nurse her boy. That would be fun for me. I think I have scribbled enough. Hoping to meet you in health and prosperity, I bid you good by from your devoted husband.

D.B. White

DEAR WIFE

Mrs. Daniel B. White
Downsville, Delaware County, NY

Hilton Head, SC
Wednesday, March 29, 1865

Dear Wife,

I seat myself again to pen a few lines to you. You will think perhaps I write often. Well, I suppose I do, but who cares. If you cannot find time to read all my letters, I will write to someone else.

I cannot tell you that I feel verry nice today for I have a pain in my head. I have had a severe cold for some time. My head is badly stopped up part of the time for the past four or five weeks. I have been nearly as deaf as Uncle Johnney Holmes was. I am better than I was, and think that I shall be all right again as soon as I get rid of my cold. I do not feel any uneasy about it, but it is verry inconvenient. To be deprived of our facualties teaches us the worth of them. We would hardly know the worth of health should we never be sick. War teaches us to prize the blessing of peace.

You inform me that your eyes trouble you considerably. I feel some anxious about it. I fear you will never have as strong eyes as you had before you had the inflamation in them, but I hope you will be careful and not task the facualty of seeing too much, then they may get strong again.

You seem to have made up your mind to stay at home this summer. Well, I had rather have you do so than otherwise.

Nett thought she would live with Mr. Purdy. I can say something about that arangement. I think she ought to have 12 shillings a week at least and a little more if possible. She thought perhaps she could have done better at Warren's, if she could have managed to catch Duwit. I do not know him; I think I saw him several times at Downsville last summer, and he tipped the glass a little freely. If I were a girl and wanted to catch a fine sort of a fellow for a man, I should not regret the loss of one summer if I could catch either John or George Warren. They are fine boys.

J.D. Scott is Chief of Police in a Nigger town about a mile from here. He stays here and goes over there evry day to see how the wenches get along. The name of the town is Mitchelville. I do not think I have mentioned the place to you before.

Geo. Barber is well and enquires after you often. I have heard nuthing from Wm. Christie for the past winter. Where is he, and what is he doing?

Nett has not forgotten Frasier's kindness, yet she feels rough and she may have reasons for so doing.

DEAR WIFE

You speak of meeting Mr. & Mrs. Neish at Downsville and that you was glad to see them. I would be happy to see Betsy too.

You say nuthing about money. Have you any, or do you stand in need of some? If so, write and I will make arangements to get some for you. I think I shall have some if I live to get mustered out of the U.S. service, perhaps I shall not get any before. I see no signs to convince me that we will get paid before. We see the inconvenience of not having some of the green backs verry often, I think.

I shall close for the present. You will think this a miserable substitute for a letter, but I do not feel like writing today. I have t'other end foremost, and I guess some are upside down.

You wanted to know whether I was joking or just in fun about enlisting again. A little of both is my answer.

You must write often and send those pictures as soon as convenient. I remain as ever your sincere husband.

D.B. White

In March, 1865 Sherman's armies were on the move through North Carolina. Battles were fought at Kinston, Averasborough, and Bentonville, and on the 23rd Sherman reached Goldsboro, only a few days behind schedule. At

THE DESERTERS

Goldsboro, he met another Union army, under the command of General Schofield, which had moved westward from the coast to join him. Sherman's force now numbered close to 100,000 men. General Lee wrote to President Davis, "I fear now it will be impossible to prevent a junction between Grant and Sherman...."

During the final days of March the Union attack on Petersburg and Richmond began. General Grant, with 125,000 men, faced General Lee, whose armies counted less than a third that number. Lee knew he would eventually have to withdraw. He planned to wait until early April when drier roads would make it easier to pull back, and then join General Joseph E. Johnston who now commanded all the Confederate forces south of Richmond.

On Monday, April 3rd, Union forces captured Richmond and Petersburg.

Mrs. Daniel B. White
Downsville, Delaware County, NY

           Hilton Head, SC
         Monday, April 3, 1865

Dear Wife,

  I Take pen in hand once more to pen a few lines to you. I am happy to be able to say that I am well & sincerely hope these lines may find you & all our friends enjoying the same blessings.

I have received no mail from home since I last wrote to you, but the mail boat was due yesterday, & she will shurely come before long. The mail boat is anxiously watched. We all keep time for her, but she takes her own time.

There is no news, only some changes in our company officers. I wrote to you a short time since concerning officers, comish. & noncomish., who I expected would be promoted, but changes was made that was unexpected to us.

Frank Campbell was First Sargent and entitled to Orderly. J.D. Scott was Second Sargent. W.R. Stevens was Third Sargent, and he is promoted over Frank & Scott, and is Orderly of Co. K now. So far as I am concerned, I care but little, but all the old soldiers & part of the recruits feel verry rough about it. They generally feel that it is Frank's place & that he is the most capable of the two as far as doing the business is concerned. I fear with the present feeling that exists in the Company, W.R. Stevens will be likely to have rather an unpleasant time. Ruswell has always used me well, so I shall take no side against him.

George Barber was First Corporal and entitled to the first promotion, but they saw fit to jump Mark Hanford over him, so Mark is Sergt. instead of Barber. We all see the injustice of those promotions, or think we see injustice, but the commissioned officers have the power to promote whom they please. George alows that he would rather not be promoted if he has to show any superior authority over the boys more than what his duty requires or wipe officer's a__ses for the sake of promotion, and I am shure the boys in the Company think just as much of those that are jumped as they would have done had they been promoted as they were entitled to have been.

We still remain in the Yard. We have been inspected evry day or two for the past week by officers from the regiment. They seem to be verry anxious about us and find fault if possible. It is reported that either Co. D or K will have to go back to camp, & give room for Co. C, as they seem to be bound to have Company C here. Well let them work at it. A short time will decide the question now I think.

I have no more news to write until after the mail comes. I might inform you that those boys on the boat are detached, and will be likely to stay their time out there.

Yours as ever,
D.B. White

Tuesday, April 4, 1865

Dear Wife,

I received a letter from you today, and was glad to hear that you were well. I am well, and have to start for Jacksonville,

Florida with some men, so I will bid you good by, & write soon again.

Mrs. Daniel B. White
Downsville, Delaware County, NY

Hilton Head, SC
Tuesday, April 4, 1865

Dear Wife,

You may be surprised a little should you read a letter I hastily directed to you this afternoon and then read this dated the same day, but a little later date. I was detailed to go to Jacksonville, Fla. with a squad of men & ordered to report amediately. I thought that half finished letter would be better than none & I should not return in time to send any letter by the next mail.

I got all ready to start, but the men were not ready, and Oliver Washburn came to me and was verry anxious to go in my place. He alowed he would rather give five Dolls. than not go. He had no $5.00 to give, and I told him I did not want his money, but thought as I was ready to go, I should not give it up, but he begged so hard I finaly told him to go.

THE DESERTERS

I cared but little except to see the place, & there was four others going from our company. Jacksonville is 12 or 15 hours run from here, and was one of the 144th's old stopping places. If I had not taken Oliver's place on guard, I could've had a chance to go to Charleston. I am going there the first opurtunity I have to see the place, I might say the cradle of the rebellion & sesesion were fostered in, but the infant sesesion has run away.

I was happy to get a letter from you today. I felt disapointed when I saw where it was mailed, still I thought the handwriting was yours.

I received a letter from Magie White. She informed me that they were well & Nelly had another daughter. That was not news to me, but it was just as well she thought it would be. She informed me that she had received a letter from you, and that Mother was over there then.

The only fault I could find with yours was the brevity. I do like to have long communications with you. Your love & devotion I never doubt, but smile at your simplicity. Sometimes I think I have learned to love you more than ever I did, if such a thing were possible, within the past six months. How often I have looked over the six months previous to leaving home with bird's eye view. I can see times I teased you just for fun & made you feel uncomfortable because you thought I was in earnest. I used to like to see you pout a little sometimes, but I was unkind to you in doing so. How many men before me have done the same thing just for fun & it turned out in earnest after a while, and made two mortal beings unhappy for a lifetime. I have often read in story that woman never looked more beautiful than when she pouted just a little.

I do not think you was ever angry at me for teasing you, but I often think you saw the dangerous effect that might arise from my shortsightedness in so doing. But enough, forgive me for the past; trust me in the future. God bless you & protect you, & I will too, may kind Heaven grant me the priveledge of meeting you again on earth.

You said our folks were all well, and that they were preparing to go down the river, that John had hired to work for Bates. He gets big wages, & I hope he will like his place & get his pay all right.

You said that you was visiting before Nett went away from home, but did not say where she was going. I took it from her last letter that she intended to live at Purdy's this summer. I hope you have had a pleasant visit. I am shure they would all be kind to you.

I hope brother William may live to be with his family again. It must be hard to leave a family of small children.

I must go to the guard house now. I will bid you an affectionate good night. Finish this tomorrow if I have my health & life spared me.

THE DESERTERS

Yours as ever,
D.B. White

Hilton Head, SC
Wednesday, April 5, 1865

Dear Wife,

 I take pen in hand once more to write a few more lines to you. I am well today, & hope you are enjoying the same blessing. I have a miserable pen to write with, and borowed at that. I think you will be apt to say I must have been excited yesterday when you see the style of writing I done. I might have been, but I think I never had a cooler nerve in my life.

 I have written an answer to Magie's letter, and will finish the second to you. That will sum up my writing for the present week. If only I had some news to write it would not be a hard task, but to try to make news requires some headwork.

 You informed me that you had received the books I sent. You seem to think soldiers should not be so wicked with such good books to read. Dear friend, a great many soldiers do not care to read such altho there is but few that can resist their influence at times. Some sketch or anecdote of some great General's name atached will atract attention. After the anecdote comes the moral. Who can read one part of a story that has atracted atention and drop it without reading the whole.

I do think the Christian Commission has & will do a great deal of good in our land. The soldier's friend they have proved to be in many cases. There is a Christian Commission office at Hilton Head. They distribute a great deal of reading matter amongst us. They invite the soldier to come to the office, give him pen, ink, & paper if he chooses to write, without charge. The Reb prisoners often used to say, "We will often think of the Christian Commission & remember their kindness. Should we despise all other Northern institutions, we will bless the Christian Commission." Clothing, eatables, dainties of many kinds are given to the needy.

I wrote a letter to Mrs. Daniel Frasier some time ago, but have received no answer. You should not feel so hard against her. Perhaps she is not to blame for not going home. How can she do so contrary to the wishes of her lord & master. She is placed in a position where she cannot do just as she might wish to. It is better to submit sometimes rather than to have trouble about matters where it might be avoided.

I was interupted this afternoon in writing & shall close this evening. Samuel Blair from Co. E came to make me a visit. He is my cousin, and has been nearly all winter at the hospital sick, but looks healthy now. I was verry glad to see him looking so well again.

We see no signs of getting pay yet. Perhaps we will not until our time is out. It will be uncomfortable, but we are used to being without money so it will not come so hard as it did a while ago.

It is just five months before my time should be out. Seven months ago today I dressed myself in Uncle Sam's clothes. The next 5 looks longer than the past 7, but if it should please God to bless me with health & spare my life, the time will soon pass away.

I must bid you good by for the present. I would like to write more, but space will not permit. Heaven protect you & all my dear friends, & I remain your sincere husband.

D.B. White

Mrs. Daniel B. White
Downsville, Delaware County, NY

Hilton Head, SC
Sunday, April 9, 1865

Dear Wife,

I take pen in hand once more to pen a few lines to you. I am happy to be able to inform you that I am well & trust these lines may find you all enjoying the same blessing. Not being on guard today, I thought I would spend a little time conversing with you.

All the news I have to write is the reported capture of Richmond. You will conclude that I must think you are not posted or I should not take the trouble to write what you will undoubtedly know long before this reaches you, but there is some news you would not be likely to learn from newspapers. There was a salute fired from the fort at Hilton Head of one hundred guns, all that done by Co. E boys at or near noon today.

Also, there was a woman arested in the Yard this morning wearing man's aparel. She came with a squad from Savannah, ariving here last night. She may be a noted caracter; perhaps the least said about caracter the better for her. She claims that there is two more of her style in the same squad. If so, we do not find them yet.

It is raining some today. Perhaps we are going to have a break up, and freshet soon. Whether it will make out to freshen all the salt water in the harbour remains to be seen.

The boys that were to St. Augustine, Jacksonville, Savannah, and Charleston have all returned. I do not mean any that were on the gun boats, those are excepted, as I learn they are detached from the Company.

THE DESERTERS

The boys in the Company are all quite well, and we maintain our position altho the Col. & Capt. [Matthew C.] Lewis do not alow us to do so in peace. Capt. Lewis wants to take the Provost duty to do by the job and have his Co. do the duty and he be Provo Martial. Bully for him, I say. I have heard that Gen. Littlefield told the Colonel a few days ago that he would like to have him mind his own business, and when he saw fit to send us back, he would do so. The 144th have moved their camp from the old ground, and are nearer our quarters than before. If that comforts them any, I am willing they should have all the comfort they can, but I do not feel like giving up the ship to them yet.

I hope the war will be ended before we move, and then I want to move pretty quick, but I fear that the war will last some time yet. I can hardly see the end, yet if I should listen I might hear it perhaps for I can hear about as good as ever I did at present. I am getting rid of that awful cold that has been my greatest trouble for the past two months.

Some of the young thoughtless boys of Co. K have had a great mind to marry lately. They have asociated with some of those refugee girls, and became enamoured with them. One man belonging to Co. K was married to a refugee woman some time ago. That was the starting point. I think lovemaking and matrimony will play out. The Captain thinks it his duty to interfere in such cases. All those concerned in those afairs are old soldiers and young boys at that. I think they have forgoten our lovely Northern Lasses and respect for friends and themselves in acting as they do or would like to do. I can see but little about any Southron girl that I have seen to atract the fancy, so far at least.

I shall have to close for the present. Should it stop raining I intend to go to church this evening to hear a Catholic minister preach. There is a Catholic church in this place, and there is preaching twice on Sunday at the Soldier's Rest. I have not been to church for some time, being on duty evry Sunday.

Yours in love,
D.B. White

Wednesday, April 12, 1865

Dear Wife,

I seat myself this morning for the purpose of penning a few lines to you. I received a verry kind & welcome letter from you this morning, & you may feel asured that I was happy to hear from you & to hear that you was well & all my friends were enjoying the same blessing.

I received letters from John Merritt, J. White, and Mrs. Frasier. I am thankful to hear from all my friends, and it gives me sincere pleasure to hear that all are enjoying good health.

THE DESERTERS

Margaret wrote a verry kind letter to me. She alows that she has not forgoten her old friends, and would be happy to see them all, but circumstances will not admit of her leaving home and children at present, but hopes to do so as soon as circumstances will admit.

If you knew the pleasure it afoards me to hear from you and to read your verry kind letters, you would not begrudge the time you spend in writing me.

I am happy to hear that our folks have got their lumber safely down the river and that they are likely to get a good price for it. They have had trouble enough with it. I have heard that lumber was selling as low as $10 & 12 per thousand. I hope our folks sold theirs before it came down so low.

James informed me that he had been boiling sap all day and wrote to me in the evening. He says that those that had good camps would make lots of shugar. I wish I could have an opurtunity to eat about one pound of it warm.

I was up to camp last night, and saw several of the boys. They are geting along finely. William Johnston is well, and I presume he has not forgotten the time we had with Beatie. I recolect having cold fingers that morning.

You seem bent on hiring out. I shall say nuthing more about it. You already know my feelings concerning that matter, and I think you will be a goose to hire out at all, and if you do to take $2.00 per weak to do the same work you could just as well have 18 or 20 shillings for. I have hired out before now on conditions to do such and such work for different prices, and always regreted taking a little less on acount of having it a little easier. I always found that what was to do had to be done the same, and different prices made but little difference with me. If you had to hire out, the only objection I should make to your working for George Fuller would be the late and iregular hours that it is nesesary to be up and round at.

H. Gray is not here, so I cannot tell him of the marriage of his sister. I have not seen Hiram in over two months; he is on the boat. Buell is there yet. I have not heard from him in some time.

We had another wedding in Co. K last Monday night. There was another apointed for Tuesday night, but the Domanie refused to marry them. There are several more from the regiment and one or two more from Co. K apointed. Perhaps you would like to hear what I think about the boys marrying these Southron blosoms.

I will tell you what I think. I think they disgrace themselves, their friends, their company, and regiment and common country. I think the women as a general thing are of the lowest class, a disgrace to their sex. What worthy

THE DESERTERS

woman would take up with strangers as they have. The boys are either young or regardless of their own good name. For some of them, I feel sorry, for I think they have been deceived. Now how is this afair to end when the regiment's time is out. I do not think any of them will wish to stay here, neither will they want to take their women north with them. What will be the consequence. No decent girl will wish their company after they get home. A life of misery will be the inevitable result.

I shall close for the present, and if I am not detailed to go off on a boat with men today, I shall write again before the mail boat leaves. You must write often. Give my respects to all, and I remain as ever your sincere friend and husband.

D.B. White

Mrs. Daniel B. White
Downsville, Delaware County, NY

          Hilton Head, SC
         Friday, April 14, 1865

Dear Wife,

I take the present opurtunity of writing a few aditional lines to you. I am happy to be able to inform you that I am well, & sincerely hope this may find you all as well as it leaves me.

I regret to say I must inform you of the death of William Elwood. He died at the hospital night before last about 8 o'clock. He was burried yesterday. Several of the boys of Co. K were at his funeral. I could not go, being on duty.

Our officers from this place are nearly all at Charleston today to hear a speech from the Rev. Henry Ward Beecher and witness the ceremony of raising the flag on Fort Sumter. You no doubt have read the arangements in the last week's newspaper. I think if they had contributed the amount which will be spent on the ocasion toward aleviating the sufferings of the widows and orphans of soldiers who have fallen in the service of their country, it would have been a godsend to many a sufferer.

Well Amanda, I have written a letter to Mr. & Mrs. Frasier. I wrote to John. You may ask him if he will not let you read it. I presume he will not do so. I talked verry plain to him. I should not have said the same to any other person. He tried to creep round my meaning in writing as I did before, but I saw that he fully understood the meaning of my remarks.

Well now Amanda, if I had any news to write it would lessen my task greatly. You did not say much about your visit in the clove. I guess you did not enjoy yourself verry good. Perhaps you were in so much trouble about shugar making that you could not content yourself anywhere.

We do not get any pay yet; neither do I know when we will. We get along verry well with good health, but army rations are rough for a sick person. I trust we will not need to live on army rations after we get our time in, for I think war will be no more before autum leaves fall again. I have had the best of health for some time past. If I am blessed with good health what more can I ask for.

I will give you a short detail of matrimonial afairs in Company K. You will think I am lost to friends at home should the fever continue to rage in Co. K as it has for the past month. I will give you names altho that will be but little satisfaction for you do not know many of the boys that have fell through the seat of their breeches and hung themselves: James Elderkin, James Seath, John Stevens, Edward Gransbury, James Bush, Alex Golden. Don't you think that is enough to condemn Co. K, having so many Government women transferred into it. All that is likely to save Dick Spencer will be that he is a little too reserved for the ladies he would have to deal with.

Our respectable boys comes down on those weddings rough. They claim the right to be respected as a company at least, and those weddings are a disgrace to all members.

DEAR WIFE

I shall send Margaret's letter inside of this. You must lay it by for me to refer to when I may have the priveledge of meeting you again. Do not make a public thing of any of the contents.

I must bid you good by. God bless you and preserve us both, and I remain as ever, your true and sincere husband.

D.B. White

Mrs. Daniel B. White
Downsville, Delaware County, NY

Hilton Head, SC
Tuesday, April 18, 1865

Dear Wife,

With pleasure I seat myself once more to pen a few lines to you. I received your verry welcome letter this morning. What cause to be thankful I have, my dear friends all enjoying good health. What better news could I get.

War news of the highest importance. What glorious news from the Army, but all sweets have their bitter, I think. After we are in receipt of such good news, then the news of

President Lincoln being assasinated. The same atempt made to take the lives of others holding positions of the highest order in our National afairs casts a gloom over our land. God's just retribution must follow in the steps of such a desperado, & fall on the heads of all concerned in such hellish & cowardly act.

The mail boat arived yesterday about 3 o'clock. Flags were amediately lowered to a half mast. The apearance today, things look gloomy enough. Flags at half mast and drooping. A gun is fired evry half hour from the forts & each gun boat in honour to the memory of our deceased President. What may be the end of such treason & inhuman acts God only knows, but I feel willing to leave the issue in his hands. Vengence is mine saith the Lord; I will repay it.

Business is suspended, public and government buildings dressed in mourning. What a contrast between the few past days & today. All was ambition & show; all today in mourning. Such is life. Today we may see cause for joy; tomorrow sorrow may brood over our spirits and cast gloom over our whole future life.

I received a letter from James. He stated that they were all well, and that he had been in the hollow. He informed me that James Nichol had lost an arm in the present battle before Petersburg, and one of his legs was seriously injured. How often has friends been shocked by hearing such news from friends in the Army for the past four years. May war soon be as amongst the things of the past, and sweet peace smile on our dear land once more.

I am shure Mrs. Patterson would feel verry bad when she heard of the death of her husband. We can sympathize with bereaved friends, but we know but little of their feelings until death comes home. Then reality shows us how light & indifferent have been our feelings & sympathies in behalf of our fellow creatures.

We are all in about the same position we have been for some time past. Several of our boys go to the Doctor for prescriptions. The weather is verry warm, and the boys are troubled a good deal with diarrhea George Barber has been off the hooks for some time, almost a week.

I will close for the present, and write some more before the mail goes out. Good by.

Friday, April 21, 1865

I seat myself for a few minutes again to finish this would be letter. I have nuthing new to write.

I will inform you that we had inspection yesterday, were inspected by the Inspector General. I guess he was well suited with our style, he apeared to be at least.

THE DESERTERS

The boys in the company are rather better today, generally taking us all on an average, as Gilbert used to say.

I presume you are having considerable stirring times about now. Jim informed me that they had tapped the shugar bush. You will be out of that trouble now, and I am glad you have had a chance to work at shugar making. Well, save me a hunk, and if you see Polly Jane, tell her if she does not save me some 'lasses on a chip I will be verry apt to give her the mitten.

I have found the girl I have been looking for at last. She came in the Yard last night. I have not talked to her yet, but I saw her fifteen or twenty rods distant, and just made up my mind to marry her if she would have me. I tell you she is a glinter. I am going to see her as soon as I finish writing. I will inform you as to my success in my next [letter].

George Barber is round all right again.

You seem to have a good deal of trouble about my headache. I did a while too, but I do not see any trouble about it now. I have been verry healthy for a long time now.

I am glad you have had a letter from Margaret. You will perhaps see that you was too fast judging her.

I guess I shall have to close for I have written all I know. You can tell James I was glad to hear from him. I may not have time to write to him at present, but I will do so soon.

DEAR WIFE

I guess George will not write to me any more. I wrote to him some time since, and have not received no answer.

I have not seen H. Tiffany for some time, but I heard yesterday that he is feeling bad enough. Sam Babcock read a letter that he had received from home to Henry, giving him a detail of matters concerning his wife. Henry has received no letters from home for some time.

I will close for the present hoping this miserable letter may find you all enjoying the best of health, and may hope be implanted strong enough to give you courage to battle with the future.

Write often. My respects to all, and I remain your true husband.

D.B. White

Mrs. Daniel B. White
Downsville, Delaware County, NY

Hilton Head, SC
Thursday, April 27, 1865

Dear Wife,

THE DESERTERS

I seat myself once more for the purpose of penning a few lines to you to inform you that I am quite well at present, & I hope this may find you all well. I received my mail an hour or two since, & was verry glad to hear from you & to hear that you were all well.

I received letters from J. McLarren, George Merritt, Nett, and yourself, and received good news from all. I thought I would commense answering them fourthwith, as I will most likely be on guard tomorow and shall have to improve my time or not be able to answer all before the mail closes again.

I have no news to write, consequently my letters will be brief; nuthing new at the Head. The acount of the escape, for the present at least, of [General] Joe Johnston, his army, and the probable escape of [President] Jeff Davis causes quite a sensation. We all supposed Joe Johnston had surrendred to General Sherman, and looked at war as about played out. It has been reported that a force of 25 or 30 guerrillas have been seen on this Island, and have burned some Niger shanties. I don't believe the report, altho it may be possible.

Our Lt. Colonel [Calvin A. Rice] tried to startle us last night. He came here and gave orders to have all guards at the guard house to be in readiness to fall out at a moment's warning, and directed the Orderlies of Co. D & K to wake us all up, and prepare to be in readiness to fall out, and rather fall in, at any moment. This order came about midnight. Some got up, some did not. None seemed to be verry badly scared. One of the boys in Company K had a violent atack of the belly ache. I got up, loaded my cartridge box, and went to bed again, and slept verry soundly. This morning proved the orders to be a farce of the Colonel's.

I shall have to stop for supper is ready. I shall write more tonight.

I now take pen in hand again. I was much pleased to get so long a letter, or part of two.

Nett comes back on you rather rough. She says she was ready and anxious to acompany you to Downsville to have your fotographs taken, but you had on one of your spells and would not go with her. I was sorry to hear that you and her did not agree to go at one time, as she seems to think she will not go with you at any future time, and I shall be the one that will be disapointed in the end.

George informs me that he had returned from down the river, had sold the lumber for a good price, but I presume he purposely omitted to state the price he sold for.

Newton Holmes came back on the mail boat, was here this morning. He said all the folks were well at home, and that he had a verry pleasant trip.

I will have to return my sincere thanks to you for the green back money you was so kind as to send to me. I had not seen any in so long a time, I do not know what I shall do with it. I could get a bottle of whiskey for three dollars, & I do not know whether I can get half a bottle or not. I will enquire about it as soon as I can have an oportunity.

You seem to be pretty well posted in reference to the situation of hens, sheepses and cows, and even go so far as to include women. I hope they all do well, increase and replenish the earth.

I have not received any letters from Nett White or any of the family.

Newton Holmes brought letters for several of the boys, brought Honor's likeness for Ruswell and Jane's for Buell. I have not heard from the boat boys in some time.

I shall close for the present, and remain your true friend.

D.B. White

Mrs. Daniel B. White
Downsville, Delaware County, NY

Hilton Head, SC
Friday, April 28, 1865

Dear Wife,

I take the opurtunity to write a few aditional lines to you. I am feeling just about middling good today. I have been off the hooks a little for a few days past, but have not taken any of the Doctor's poison. I do not want to play off duty, & take any of their quinine. When I am so sick I am obliged to them, it will make out to be a different case.

My girl that I spoke about in my last [letter] only staid here a short time, and went to New York, so I am just put back on my old ground again. A course of true love never did run smooth.

I don't want you to commense a story & leave it untold as you did in your last in speaking of your conversation with Newton Holmes. If you start curiosity, settle it by telling the whole story.

I do not think you have as much money as you stand in need of. If you have not, inform me. I can suply you much better than I can myself. I had my mind made up when I left home never to send for any money on any acount, but I have seen times to make me think of money as a necesity. We can get writing paper & envelopes from the sutler by paying exorbitant prices, but it takes greenbacks to buy postage stamps. I have saved all my money for that purpose, & have some left yet.

THE DESERTERS

I used to tell you how easily I could eat my rations. Since warm weather set in, one loaf of bread will last me two or three days. It used to take about two loaves for one day. Verry few of the boys eat any pork or fresh beef any more.

I have had a pretty good twist of chronic diarrhea but I am nearly right again.

I do not know that I can write any news. I shall have to close for the present, but will write a few lines before mailing this.

Saturday, April 29, 1865

I have been hard at work all day, & am not through yet, but have an opurtunity to send this to town to mail. We are fixing up for a right smart inspection tomorow. I am feeling tolerable good, but am tired [of] scouring and cleaning.

I presume I have omitted to write some things I intended to, but I shall try to find more time the next mail.

I shall try to answer George's if possible. If he does not get any letter from me, you can tell him the reason.

I should like to answer Jimmies, but shall have to put it off for the present. I send my love to all. I wish your father could write to me. I should like to see the old fellow right well.

DEAR WIFE

You will think I am getting so careless I will write so poorly, soon you cannot read it at all. I do not take the pains I should, but when I write to the girls I put on the airs. You must consider where those remarks came from, and then they will be overlooked.

I remain your sincere & loving husband.

D.B. White

On Sunday, April 9, 1865, General Robert E. Lee surrendered his Army of Northern Virginia to General Grant at Appomattox Court House. His tired, hungry, vastly outnumbered army could no longer continue. Grant was as generous in his surrender terms as President Lincoln would allow. Confederate officers could keep their sidearms, and both officers and men could retain their horses. It was time for spring planting, and the horses would be needed. Grant also arranged for the feeding of Lee's men from Union stores, a provision which graphically illustrates the wretched state of the Confederate army at that time.

In his letter of April 14th, Daniel wrote about the celebration at Charleston and Fort Sumter. General Robert Anderson, who had surrendered Fort Sumter four years earlier, raised the Union Flag. Henry Ward Beecher spoke, the 144th regimental band played, and there were fireworks in the evening. Little did anyone think that President Lincoln would be assassinated that night.

THE DESERTERS

The troops at Hilton Head learned of Lincoln's death on April 17th. They had been in good spirits, "All was ambition and show....", but now a gloom settled over the place, as indeed it did over much of the country. General Joseph E. Johnston, meeting with General Sherman to negotiate the surrender of his armies called it, "a great calamity to the South." Southern leaders knew what they could expect from Lincoln in the way of reconstruction, but feared his weaker-willed successor, Andrew Johnson.

On the 18th, near Durham Station, North Carolina, General's Sherman and Johnston signed a surrender document. This memorandum went far beyond either general's authority. It not only described the terms of surrender, but also outlined peace between the North and South. Sherman claimed later that he had not received President Lincoln's order back in March to only go so far as to secure a surrender.

Sherman's agreement was rejected by President Johnson, and on April 26th General Johnston surrendered under terms very similar to those reached by Grant and Lee at Appomattox.

Pockets of Confederate troops were surrendering all throughout the south. In May it was all over.

Daniel left Hilton Head for the first time since his arrival there in September, 1864. After depositing the prisoners under his care with the Provost Martial in New York City, he made his way to Downsville to spend a short furlough with Amanda, then traveled back to Hilton Head. The 144th was preparing to go home.

CHAPTER SIX

SURRENDER AND HOME

Mrs. Daniel B. White
Downsville, Delaware County, NY

> Hilton Head, SC
> Friday, May 5, 1865

Dear Wife,

I take pen in hand to write a few more lines to you to inform you that I am well, & hope this may find you all as well as yours found me. I received yours of April 24th this morning. I take pleasure in answering it. The greatest comfort I have is reading letters from friends, & answering the same.

I received letters from Ann, Sarah, & Maggie White, and received a letter from James a couple of days since. It is a great pleasure to hear from home and hear that all that are near & dear are well. I am verry anxious to hear from William [White] since the battle at Petersburg.

Maggie informed me that James Nichol was dead. That is sorry news for his folks, but so it has been for the past four years. So may Heaven grant that the days of strife & bloodshed are at an end. We all look at the war as virtually at an end. The work of death & deavastation has closed. The work of reconstruction must begin. May wisdom prevail in our councils. May officers holding offices of trust and responsibility be impresed with a sense of their responsibility to God & man. May the rights of man be one of the first considerations.

We have fought Rebels in the South & traitors in the North, & have conquered both, but our duty to our country does not end there. We must watch with vigilence. Our past indifference caused us seas of blood & millions of treasure to say nuthing of cripples for life, widows & orphans without number, but I trust the past may prove a warning in the future.

You seem to think the death of Lincoln is no greater loss than the death of many others that have fallen, but I think otherwise. The position he occupied in our nation as Chief Magistrate was a verry serious afair. I do not think his assasin did not kill him from personal feelings of revenge, but a feeling of revenge against the government. If it had been personal, the assasin & colleagues conected with him would not have been likely to atempt the destruction of other officials high in authority as government officials, but you was right in some of your asertions that life to him was no sweeter than many a poor private who has fallen for his country. He was no nearer or dearer to his family than others. The calamnity to his family was not as serious as it has been in many cases where a poor family were dependant on the father for support.

I will close for supper.

You inform me than your Uncle Olliver was sick, & that your mother was away from home. I hope Olliver may be restored to health, and that you & Nett will not tear the house down before she gets home.

I am with you when you say that Nett is an awful girl, but I like to hear her express her sentiments, if they prove rather rough at times.

I do not think John could, with consistency, come back on me verry bad, for I told him the truth.

I have been convinced for some time past that your father was my friend. I am sorry to hear that he sometimes forgets that inebriation punishes the transgresor in nearly evry case, but we must overlook his faults & cherish his virtues. I am sorry to look back on the past and take into consideration the hard labour he has performed and the small amount he has for a recompense. He has been honest I believe, so far as circumstances would admit, with all men, and has trusted too much to the honesty of others. Their lumber matters have come out just as I feared, but I trust changes for the better may soon occur. Your father has done well sawing this spring, and he always does well when there is work to perform.

I hope I may not lose the next letter from Nett if I am to receive her fotograph and yours; I trust may come all right. I will try to write to James & Charley this mail.

Our boys talk all the time now about being discharged & going home to hold the 4th, but I do not flatter myself that such will be the case. I should like to get rid of staying here during the warm weather.

Several from the regiment have gone to the hospital in order to get their discharge. One man from our Co. went to the hospital. All that are in hospitals & those not fit for amediate duty are to be discharged amediately.

I suppose you have had an early spring, but you do not have ripe blackberries yet, & we do, if we are a mind to go and pick them. The weather has not been as warm for the past week as before. We had a couple of weeks verry warm weather.

I shall close for the present. I often forget to answer questions, and think of it after it is too late. Nett wanted me to send her some shell. I shall try to do so. I think some of us will send a box home soon with the blankets & other clothing. If we should, I shall try to send her some shells. I cannot get them as nice here as on the other side of the harbour.

You infer, as I take it, that so often as I send two sheets in one envelope, you have to pay extra postage. How is it? You must write often. Mail has reached me verry regular for some time past.

My love to all, and I remain as ever, your affectionate & loving husband.

D.B. White

United States Sanitary Commission
Soldier's Letter
New York City Postmark   May 14, 1865

Mrs. Daniel B. White
Downsville, Delaware County, NY

Soldier's Home
New York City
Sunday, May 14, 1865

Dear Wife,

SURRENDER AND HOME

I seat myself again this morning to pen a few lines to you to inform you that I am well, and sincerely hope these lines may find you all well.

You will doubtless be surprised to learn that I am here. I left Hilton Head last Tuesday noon, ariving here Friday. I did not know scarcely one hour before leaving that I was coming. One Corporal from Co. D, James M. Dibble, and myself were sent here with two prisoners. We reported them all right at the Provost Martial's in this city, and if we had been blessed with means sufficient to pay our fare, would have been home with you today.

We tried yesterday to raise the soap, but did not succeed. We expect to start for Hilton Head again Tuesday on board the steamer Fulton. I think we will all be home in a month or two.

The Soldier's Home is crowded with discharged men and men waiting to be discharged.

The boys were all pretty well when we left them. If I should stay here longer than until Tuesday, I will inform you.

I must close; hoping to reach home soon.

From your ever devoted and loving husband,
D.B. White

DEAR WIFE

Mrs. Daniel B. White
Downsville, Delaware County, NY

Hilton Head, SC
Tuesday, May 30, 1865

Dear Wife,

I seat myself to pen a few lines to you. I arived here last Sunday night. We had a rough passage, but all came out safe.

The health of the boys is not so good as when we left them, still none are dangerous. I think all is excitement here about going home, but I see but little change since I left.

The Seventh Regt. of Regulars came here as they calculated to relieve our regiment, but were sent to Savannah, but there is part of a regiment here who intend to do duty here in a few days. They are the 9th Connecticut.

I do not suffer with the heat since I came back, but feel more comfortable than when at home. Do not worry about our coming home. Time will bring us, but how much time I cannot tell.

We expect pay before long, as the money came on the boat when we did, to pay troops in the Department.

Tell all the folks I send my respects to them, but shall make short letters this time.

I found Net's likeness all right & several other letters, one from Mary and Nett White.

From your affectionate husband,
D.B. White

Thursday, June 1, 1865

Dear Wife,

I am quite well, and was on guard yesterday.

The boat is lying here longer than usual, what for I cannot tell. Company D has been relieved in the Provo Yard, and ordered to camp. One Company of the 9th Connecticut came in today in their place. The guards are all from our Company today. What these changes are for I cannot say.

I think we will stay here some time yet. I have but little time to write at present, so good by.

Yours as ever,
D.B.W.

DEAR WIFE

P.S. The weather is verry warm. The water tastes worse than ever. Write as soon as you get this. The boys are all here that was on the boats.

Mrs. Daniel B. White
Downsville, Delaware County, NY

Hilton Head, SC
Thursday, June 8, 1865

Dear Wife,

I take pen in hand to write a few lines to you once more. I am well and hope this may find you and all my friends as well as it leaves me. We have received no mail since a week ago last Monday. The last boat did not bring any.

I suppose you are all looking for us to come home soon. Well we expect to go soon. The officers have had orders to have our muster out rolls ready as soon as possible. It has been talked that the Fulton would lay over until next Monday to give us time to get ready, but she is to sail Saturday, and we are not going to be ready then. We may go on the next boat, which will sail a week from next Sunday if at her usual time. Whether we go then or not remains to be seen. We

SURRENDER AND HOME

expect to have to go to Delhi to receive our pay and get our discharge. We may not be home as soon as our friends expect, but I trust we will meet you all soon.

Our boys and the boys belonging to the 9th Connecticut are having trouble, but I hope it will not amount to anything serious. I suppose some on both sides is to blame. The Engineers and some of the 9th have had one fight, and several sore heads was the consequence.

Trusting that God will spare our lives to meet again, I bid you good by.

Yours as ever,
D.B. White

Daniel B. White
Co. K 144th NYSV
Hilton Head, SC

Downsville, NY
Friday, June 9, 1865

Dear Husband,

It is with pleasure that I seat myself for the purpose of informing you how we are getting along. We are all well as usual at present, but have all been about sick for the past week with bad colds, but are getting pretty much over them now. Mother has a very bad cough, but I think she will get better of it as soon as her cold leaves her entirely. Charley Cornell has got the mumps, but they don't make him sick any yet. Don't think they will unless he gets more cold with them.

Your letter of the 30 & 1 [May 30-June 1] came in due time. It came last Tuesday night to the office, and I got it Wednesday. I was very glad to hear you arived safe and sound at your journey's end. You wrote such a queer letter to me, I don't hardly know how to take it. You hardly told me whether you were sick or well. I am afraid you are not well by the way you wrote. I hope you are, and I hope if you are not well they will not keep you down there, but will send you home where I can see that you have the cair you deserve and that is the very best of cair that a man can have.

I have about given up the idea of your getting home again until your year is up, altho I was very much in hopes you would. But, thank the Lord, they can't keep you much longer at any rate, for your time is about out.

Charley Bagley's wife [Charles H. Bagley, Co. C] was here today, and she said it was the report over around Hamden that Colonel Lewis went to see one of the head officers when he was home, and got him not to discharge the

144th until theyr time was out. I hope if that is so, he will get well punished before he gets home again.

She said too that Capt. [Matthew] Lewis had married him a wife and took her back with him. I believe she said they started yesterday morning. I hope they will have a pleasant trip going to H. Head.

I want you to wish Ruswell much joy for me, and tell him it is a general report that he is married to a very wealthy sothern widow. Tell him I am very sorry he has forgotten all the likely girls in our town. I think if he is married it is for the money and not for love, but I don't believe a word of it and I never shall until you write and tell me it is so, for I think he is to nice a fellow and has too much respect for himself and his friends at home to do such a thing as marry one of them sothern women. That is my oppinion of that.

I presume you will hear long before this reaches you of the death of Mrs. Robert Scott. Isen't that a sad thing. Little did I think, when I was there, the old lady was so near her end. Oh, how bad the family must feel.

I was down to the village Wednesday. Kate and I went down and back in one day afoot. I tell you I was about cove in when I got home at night.

I saw Uncle Jacob. He is very miserable. They heard you were home, and looked for us up there. He said just as soon as you got home we must come up. I told him we would. I am afraid Uncle Jacob will not stand it long if he don't get help soon.

I also saw Jim Sprague. I tell you he looks poorly indeed. He don't look as if he could hold up his head. He looks a great deal worse than Anson Thornton did when he was home and sick with the feaver ague.

George Fuller told me that you was pretty d____d near whipped when you got to his house that night. He made lots of inquiries about you.

We have not heard from cousin Frank but once since you went back. Then he was very poorly. I want to hear from him again very much.

There is quite an excitement around here at present. There was a man found drowned just above Brock's Bridge last Monday. No one knows who he was or where he came from. As near as they could calculate he had laid in the water about three weeks, but there is nothing sertain about it.

I will close for the present as it is milking time and I have got to go milk. So, good evening.

I have been and milked two cows and washed the milk pails and it is not quite dark yet, so I thought I would write a little more tonight.

SURRENDER AND HOME

We have had a beautiful shower this afternoon, and we needed it very much as things were getting very dry. It looks very much like rain yet tonight, and a little more will not do any damage.

Good night my dear friend.
Saturday, June 10, 1865

As Charley is going down to the village, I thought I would finish this letter.

We are all well today. It has rained most all day, and is raining yet. We had a very heavy thunder shower this morning.

We were expecting John & Polly Jane & Nett & Ann over tonight, but am afraid they will not come if it don't clear off so the bushes can dry off a little. I was in hopes they could come for I am feeling rather lonely now days, more so than before you were home.

I did not go to Charlie Grey's funeral as I spoke of in my last letter.

I have written you one letter this month dated the 2 & 3, so if you get this & don't get that one, you will know I have written to you.

Have you sent me a book, the title, "Six Months in Sesesia"? There was one come last Saturday night, and John tore the paper off so I did not see the writing. I suppose it was from you of course.

So, I will have to close as Charley is in a great hurry. Write as soon as you get this. Write a good long letter of something to read. I will write again soon, so good by.

Yours in love,
A.M. White

P.S. Price Mills has got his discharge and is back to Margaretsville.

Mrs. Daniel B. White
Downsville, Delaware County, NY

Hilton Head, SC
Saturday, June 17, 1865

Well dear wife, I am in Hilton Head Island tonight, and enjoying very good health. I presume you are well, I hope so at least, and all my friends likewise.

We all expect to start for home tomorrow as our regiment was reported ready for muster out last Thursday, but the

SURRENDER AND HOME

Mustering Officer says we cannot go as he has not had time to examine the rolls, and he will not sign them until he knows they are right. When we will go is a matter of mere conjecture. We will not be likely to know anything about when we will start until we are called on to pack in short notice. The boys are all impatient.

The weather is terrible warm, the flies, fleas, and mosquitos torture us both night and day.

I have sent an Express box today, and the Arago sails tomorrow. I sent the box to J. White for I thought it would be too much trouble for you to get it from Hancock, and Express boxes or packages will go direct to Hamden on the stage.

I spoke to James when I was home about you needing some money. He said he was out at that time. If you are in need of it before I get home, you will have to inform him. He will get it for you.

Our boys are in hot water all the time now. It is reported that we have to go to Delhi to be discharged. Some want to go there, others swear they never will march from Hancock to Delhi to be made a show of. I think the Colonel wanted to have us there on the 4th of July, but he will fail in that this year.

DEAR WIFE

I would like to get home by the 10th. If I do not, I shall not be able to do much in haying this season. We will need a couple of weeks to recruit [recuperate] up in.

I shall have to close now as it is getting late and I am on guard duty today. Cheer up, the 144th are coming home sometime this season, and I hope to be with them.

From your devoted friend and husband,
Daniel B. White

P.S. W.R. [Ruswell] Stevens requested me to inform you that he is not married, neither would he be for any amount to any refugee or Southern mushroom.

Mrs. Daniel B. White
Downsville, Delaware County, NY

Elmira, NY
Wednesday, July 5, 1865

Dear Wife,

I take my pencil in hand this morning to inform you that I am well and sincerely hope this may find you all the same. All that troubles me as to health is that I had a trial of tooth pulling about three weeks ago, and had my tooth broke off and sadly mangled without taking out the roots, and my jaw and mouth has been sore ever since.

We left Hilton Head a week ago last Monday, arrived at N.Y. City Thursday night, Friday night started for Albany, arrived there Saturday morning, staid there until Monday noon, took the NY Central Railroad, arrived at Canandaigua Tuesday morning 3 o'clock, staid until four in the afternoon, arrived at Elmira about nine in the evening, and are quartered in the barracks at present.

We have been well treated since we arrived in N.Y. State, and have had a safe and pleasant trip. There is a great many incidents I would speak of, but will wait until I get home, then I should be able to give you some account of our trip.

We hope to be able to get home inside of one week. God grant that all may enjoy the pleasure of doing so and meeting kind friends. I have heard more cheering and seen more waving handkerchiefs for the last five days than in all my life before.

The Colonel was bound to have us taken to Delhi to be discharged, but has failed. I shall not dwell on matters of no account, but say simply that I have written this to let you know how I is and where I is.

So good bye. Yours as ever, and ever the same,
D.B. White

DEAR WIFE

" History of Delaware County"
1797 Illustrated New York 1880
W.W. Mensell & Co.36 Vesey St. NY, NY

"In June [1865] the regiment was ordered to proceed to Elmira, NY to be mustered out of service and paid off. That place was reached on the 4th of July, 1865, and the mustering took place July 13th.

It was the intention of the people of Delaware to give this regiment a grand reception on the 4th of July, and they would have done so had it been mustered out where it was mustered in. Instead of one general reception there were several, and each as enthusiastic as would have been the one. Each town in its turn called meetings and welcomed its returning heroes in a most enthusiastic manner.

The flags presented to the regiment at its departure for the seat of war were formally returned to the ladies of Delaware County on Tuesday August 22nd 1865 at Delhi, where they were received. The return of the flags was a time long to be remembered. Three years before the ladies had presented them, glossy and shining, and as perfect as skillful artisans could make them, into the hands that were to bear them in the face of the foe. Now they were brought back, the gilding gone, the State flag having only the fringe and the center remaining, the national colors reduced to a tattered remnant *of rags. And yet they had gained in value by the change, for every lost fragment told of the difficulties of the march and the perils of the field, of the brave men who laid down their lives, either in the wild fervid enthusiasm of battle, or in the tediousness of the hospital — laid them down not less for their country when they perished by sickness than when they fell beneath rebel bullets. When the regiment received them, the great contest seemed comparatively doubtful — it brought them back symbols of a redeemed and regenerated country, delivered from deadly and imminent peril, and purified from a deep and damning wrong. Appropriate were the services of the day in which the ladies, as at first, took a prominent part."*

Epilogue

Daniel mustered out with the 144th in July of 1865, and returned to Downsville to be reunited with his wife and family. He and Amanda lived in the Town of Colchester, then purchased a farm of 129 acres in Gregory Hollow in the Town of Hamden. Daniel's farm diaries tell us he sold large quantities of butter to local creameries, and later records give a strong indication that he used a dog-powered churn to produce his butter. A list of farm equipment sold after his death: hay making equipment, milk cans, wagons, various types of harness, helps to complete the picture of a typical small dairy farmer, the likes of which were prevalent in Delaware County until very recently.

He and Amanda had two children, John R., born in 1866, and Ulysses S. (Liss), born in 1868. A niece, Susan Frasier, also lived with them for a time.

Sometime before 1900 Daniel and Amanda moved to a house on Knox Avenue in Downsville, where Daniel listed his profession as carpenter. Liss and his wife Nettie, stayed on the farm, running it until after Daniel's death in 1905. In the autumn of 1905 Daniel's heirs sold the farm, and Amanda sold the house on Knox Avenue in December of 1906. She went to live with Liss and his wife in Tenafly, New Jersey, and family records show she died there in 1925. John, his wife Margaret, and their family lived in Brooklyn, New York.

SURRENDER AND HOME

Amanda and Daniel are buried near each other in Paige Cemetery, Downsville.

Major General John Foster, a long-time resident of Nashua, New Hampshire, involved himself in engineering work along the northeastern coast until his death in 1874.

Colonel James Lewis returned to Delaware County for a time, became a minister, and moved to Joliet, Illinois where he died on October 28, 1899.

Corneal Bennett and his wife Esther (Launt) lived in the Town of Colchester, and had at least four children. He died in 1912, and is buried in Paige Cemetery with his wife.

Buell and Jane Robinson had a farm in the Town of Colchester which they ran with the help of their five children. Buell died in Downsville on May 5, 1892.

The Hilton Head Island of Daniel's time is gone, replaced by a vacationer's paradise of expensive homes, golf courses, hotels, restaurants, and shops. The long pier where the Arago would have docked, "Robber's Row" (the commercial section of town), the hospital, the Provo Yard, and all the various quarters and official buildings have vanished. The only reminder is a small plaque commemorating Fort Walker/Welles, and it sits on private property, a part of Port Royal Plantation, inaccessible to the casual visitor.

DEAR WIFE

The one Civil War fort remaining on Hilton Head Island, Fort Mitchel, located on Skull Creek, is now a part of Hilton Head Plantation. It is an earthenwork fort very similar to what Fort Walker/Welles must have looked like, although today it is shaded by many large trees which would have not been allowed to stand during war time. Still, the visitor can gain some appreciation for the kinds of inexpensive fortifications that were in use and effective during the war.

The cemetery on Hilton Head was moved, to become a part of the National Cemetery at Beaufort, across Port Royal Sound. There the graves of William Elwood, Philo Allison, and many others of the 144th can be found among the over 7,500 Union and Confederate dead buried there, well cared for, in neat semi-circular rows, some sheltered under liveoaks hung with Spanish moss.

Delaware County, New York has changed too, though not as dramatically. Most of the small family dairy farms are gone, replaced by a few larger, more technologically efficient farming businesses. The local people still love the taste of maple syrup, drawn and boiled-down from Delaware County sugar maple trees, but not many "tap the shugar bush" anymore, preferring to buy their syrup and maple sugar from the big concerns which can process large enough quantities of sap to make it profitably.

The hollows and cloves (from the word "cleave"; to split) of Daniel's time are still there of course, but now they are *likely to shelter the vacation homes of "city people" who appreciate the year-round beauty and serenity of the Catskill Mountains and the many outdoor activities to be found there. The people of the 1990's will not likely see horse drawn sleighs moving along snow covered roads as in Daniel's time, nor experience the tense thrill of riding a raft of logs down the Delaware River on the spring freshet, bound for Philadelphia.*

Many of Daniel's regimental comrades are buried in the cemeteries of Delaware County, surrounded by their wives, children, and ancestors. Their graves have been marked by local American Legion posts with bronze plaques commemorating their special status.

We can visit their resting places, see the small flags waving on Memorial Day, walk over the battlefields of their war and attempt to visualize the horrors they saw. We can read the great histories and memoirs of that conflict to give us whatever perspective we think is important or interesting.

But here, through the letters of a common soldier to his new wife, we can begin to understand and feel the deep, and sometimes conflicting, personal emotions of an individual going off to war.

BIBLIOGRAPHY

CARSE, Robert: "Hilton Head Island in the Civil War; Department of the South", 1987 [This book contains many fine photographs of the Hilton Head area at the time of the Civil War].

DYER, Fredrick H.: "A Compendium of the War of the Rebellion"

McKEE, James Harvey: "Back in War Times; History of the 144TH New York Volunteer Infantry", 1903

MENSELL, W.W. & Co. (publisher): "History of Delaware County; 1797 Illustrated, New York, 1880; with biographical sketches and portraits of some pioneers"

SHERMAN, General William Tecumseh: "Personal Memoirs of"